THE INFORMAL CITY

The Informal City

Michel S. Laguerre

Professor of Social Anthropology
University of California at Berkeley

St. Martin's Press   New York

First published in the United States of America in 1994

Printed in Great Britain

ISBN 0–312–12209–8

Library of Congress Cataloging-in-Publication Data
Laguerre, Michel S.
The informal city / Michel S. Laguerre.
p.   cm.
Includes bibliographical references and index.
ISBN 0–312–12209–8
1. Sociology, Urban—California—San Francisco Metropolitan Area.
2. Sociology, Urban—California—Oakland Metropolitan Area.   3. City
and town life—California—San Francisco Metropolitan Area.   4. City
and town life—California—Oakland Metropolitan Area.   5. Informal
sector (Economics)—California—San Francisco Metropolitan Area.
6. Informal sector (Economics)—California—Oakland Metropolitan
Area.   I. Title.
HN80.S4L34   1994
307.76 ' 09794 ' 6—dc20
                                                        94–16010
                                                        CIP

For my nephews Michael and Steve

Contents

Introduction

In observing everyday life in the American city, one soon realizes the complexity of human behavior and the ease with which people move from formal to informal practices. The formal world of façade, language games and the public sphere hides a second world of subtleties, nuances and ruse. That this hidden dimension is pervasive throughout the institutions of urban America is both problematic and inspirational. It implies that the city dweller is constantly crossing over fields and domains of action as a way of better positioning the self in society. It indicates also that formal activities have informal aspects that must be decoded, deconstructed and analyzed in order that we can come to grips with an understanding of the urban process.

The informal arena provides a hidden space where one can stand to read the city as a social laboratory of everyday practice. The intent of this book is to identify, describe and explain the grammatical, syntactical and morphological rules and structures of that informal reality as they are inscribed, but hidden, in the textual map of the American city. It is the city of behind-the-scenes maneuvers, an informal ethos that everyone seems to participate in, although it is usually unspoken because of the highly sensitive nature (personal, sometimes unethical or perhaps illegal) of the activities carried out there that shape the formal outcome.

The originality of this book and the theory it proposes does not lie in the recognition of the existence of the informal sector – since there are already numerous essays on the informal economy – but rather in conceptualizing a range of informal practices beyond the economic realm, and in showing the structural and relational links among them and with the formal system. It forces us to theorize about the 'gray area' of social life, and in the process to show its importance and relevance to the fabric of the formal system and the multiple ways it insinuates itself in the democratic project of the West. The existence of these informal practices is paradoxical in the sense that they make possible the

smooth functioning of the formal urban system yet at times serve
as a hindrance to the achievement of ethnic and gender equality
in the pluralist environment of the American city.

Various segments of the population read the text of informal
practices differently. The kind of reading one indulges in seems to
be related to the position of the observer in society. One may
speak then of informal practices as forming a system of signification. For the person in search of employment, the informal
arena (rather than lack of experience or competence) is more
often than not the villain that prevents him from being hired. For
employees at the workplace, it is through the informal arena that
some achieve upward mobility faster than others. For the
businessman, the informal arena is his participation in the old-
boy network that is the springboard to success in his venture. For
the homeowner, it is the hiring of informal professionals that
lowers his overhead costs. For the secretary, it is participation in
an informal group that lowers the level of psychological stress at
the workplace. For those involved full time in the informal economy, it can be their primary or sole source of income. And for the
mayor of the city, it is the quickest way to get things done without going through the usual bureaucratic red tape.

Informal practices are tied to formal practices in many different
ways. Sometimes they are central and other times interstitial or
peripheral to the formal system. Changing conditions in the
formal domain may affect the informal domain, for example in
terms of expansion or constriction. In order to construct the case
of the informal city, I have identified a number of topics for
analysis.

The San Francisco-Oakland Metropolitan Area was selected as
the site of the study. The area constitutes an informal metropolis,
although formally it is a collection of larger and smaller towns. It
is an ideal informal metropolis for our study not simply because
of the high level of informal practices carried on (some of these
can be found elsewhere), but because the physical boundaries
within the region are themselves informal and because the population moves freely across the town borders. For example, San
Francisco residents cross the Bay Bridge every day to work in
Oakland or Berkeley and therefore participate in informal practices on both sides of the Bay. Berkeley residents work in San

Francisco, and Oakland residents commute daily to work or attend school in Berkeley. This constant population movement around the Bay Area for work, school, church, hospital or entertainment, along with the use of the telephone, fax and computer for informal communication across the town boundaries, has added an informal metropolitan identity to the local neighborhood or town identity. Thus we can concentrate our attention on the larger Bay Area rather than on any of its specific entities.

Chapter 1 presents a number of models of informality, discussing the strengths and positive features of some and the weaknesses of others, in the process formulating a framework for the operationalization and analysis of the concept of the informal city. A conceptualization of the informal sphere that will guide the rest of our discussion is provided as we look at it as 'a pole of a continuum' rather than as part of a dualist structure. Some conceptual distinctions between 'raw' and 'cooked' informality not only show the influence of hegemonic practices on the informal sphere, but also point to the need to redress the bias in urban historiography by factoring in the genealogy of informal urban practices as part of the formal urban process. The theory provides a hermeneutical and structural way of explaining the informal practices as being included in the formal outcome of formal practices.

Chapter 2 presents a discussion of the production and geography of informal space in the San Francisco Bay Area. It is argued that formal space is sometimes informalized for the purpose of carrying out informal activities. The safety-valve function and subjugated status of informal space is discussed. The informal city needs a spatial infrastructure for the expression of informal practices and informal space provides just this kind of support.

The informal economy in the Bay Area is discussed in Chapter 3. This economy is found not only among the lower class and the immigrants, but also across the board, and takes various shapes – from the informal carpenter, gardener or mechanic who gets paid under the table to the freelance editor using a computer at home as a work station for unregulated work to be E-mailed to a formal firm. This regulatory function of the informal economy is highlighted here.

Chapter 4 stresses the role of informality in the conduct of city politics. Focusing on municipal politics, informal practices are studied at the neighborhood level, in the administrative structure of a Bay Area city in terms of the relations between the mayor's office and state and federal authorities. The chapter unveils the mechanisms that sustain the processuality of informal political practices and suggests that to understand urban politics one must pay attention to both its formal and informal aspects.

In Chapter 5, the way in which informality insinuates itself in the apparatus of the formal firm is studied. Informality is found in hiring and training practices, in communication systems, and in the everyday managerial operation of all firms. It is located in the interstitiality of the modern firm, and so, to understand its behavior, the grammar of the interstitiality of informality is discussed.

Informality as a support system is discussed in Chapter 6. Health care practices among the Bay Area population are found to comprise a formal and an informal dimension. Some illnesses are cured at home without the help of a doctor or hospital. Here the relations of informal health care with formal medical practices or the formal health system are analyzed. Such care plays a major role in the sense that it prevents the formal system from being clogged with minor or unnecessary treatment procedures and provides an alternative and complementary avenue to the patient.

In Chapter 7, the role of informality in shaping inter-ethnic relations is discussed. The informal arena is a back alley where the discourse about the 'other' is held. It is where people test, contest or reinforce their views of the 'other'. Inter-ethnic relations are played out at two levels, formal and informal, and the informal arena yields clues for understanding the performance of face-to-face interaction in the formal arena.

The conclusion takes up the important issue of the multivocality of informality as it fulfills diverse roles and constitutes a system of signification. Various structural positions of the relations between formality and informality are presented. The book ends with an open question: in a democratic state what, ultimately, is the role of informality? It provides some with an arena where they can rehearse their dirty tricks while they present a clean face in the formal façade of society. Perhaps more fundamentally, while informality is an open avenue where individuals can take care of their personal and group needs and speed up such processes without becoming entangled in bureaucratic red tape, it nevertheless undermines the principle of fairness and equality as it helps position some individuals competitively in the formal system while at the same time denying others access to the same sources of privilege (informal group, informal communication, old-boy network).

The book is not an ethnography of urban practices in the San Francisco Bay Area but rather an attempt at theorizing some aspects of everyday life in this multi-ethnic metropolis. To this end, we conceptualize the issue of the informal sphere or arena as a key to understanding the operation of various segments of the formal system.

A number of people have helped me in the preparation of this book. Among them, informants (some of them are informal professionals and others are not) in the San Francisco Bay Area provided me with both information and their interpretation of the informal arena in the everyday life of their neighborhoods and formal offices. I want to acknowledge their contribution to this collective endeavor. For obvious reasons, names of informants and the institutions to which some of them belong are withheld. I owe a debt of gratitude to Ed Blakely and the University-Oakland Metropolitan Forum. Two grants awarded me by the Committee on Research of the University of California at Berkeley and a sabbatical leave made the completion of this research possible.

Chapters of the book were previously read at faculty seminars at the University of Manitoba (Anthropology Department and School of Architecture and Urban Planning), Université du Québec (Institut National de la Recherche Scientifique et Département des Etudes Urbaines), Université de Montréal (Anthropology Department), Boston University (Anthropology Department), University of California at Berkeley (Geography Department and Institute of Governmental Studies) and Harvard University (Anthropology Department). One chapter was presented at the annual meetings of the American Anthropological Association held in December 1992 in San Francisco.

Three chapters of the book were previously published separately: Chapter 1 as 'The Structuring of Informal Urban Practices', Working Papers No. 3–92, Série 'Recherche', Montréal, Canada: Institut National de la Recherche Scientifique, Institut d'Urbanisme de l'Université de Montréal, Département d'Etudes Urbaines et Touristiques de l'Université du Québec à Montréal and School of Urban Planning of McGill University, 1992; Chapter 3 appeared as 'The Informal Economy in the San Francisco Bay Area', Working Paper 594, Berkeley: Institute of Urban and Regional Development, University of California, 1993; Chapter 4 was published as 'Informality and Urban Politics in Oakland', Working Paper 93–7, Berkeley: Institute of Governmental Studies, University of California, 1993. An abridged version of Chapter 4 also appeared under the title 'Informal Politics has an Ethnic Flavor in the Bay Area', in Public Affairs Report vol. 34, no. 3, 1993.

While preparing this book I spent a month in residence at the Institute of Urban Studies of the University of Winnipeg, a summer in residence at the Department of Urban Planning at McGill University, and a year in the Anthropology Department at Harvard University. I want to thank particularly Mario Carvalho, Jeanne Wolfe, Hymie Rubenstein, Dick Walker, Deirdre Meintel, Friedner Wittman, James Watson, Sally Falk Moore and Michael Herzfeld for their comments. The final outcome of the book would not have been the same without the helpful scrutiny of these scholars and the audiences – including the students at Berkeley (most notably Theresa Webster and Francisco Santamarina) who took my seminar on Informal Systems – before which the drafts were presented.

1

The Informal City Approach

In reading the sociological literature on the constitution of society, one must notice that the majority of social scientists have constantly emphasized unveiling and explaining the structure of formal society. This view of things is part of the legacy of modernity, which envisioned emancipation through reason during the Enlightenment period. This Western view stresses that progress can be achieved mainly through a rational ordering of society.

Although one can learn a great deal from studies of the formal institutions of society, failure to focus on informal practices has been a major hindrance to our understanding of the operation, ramifications and elastic contours of everyday life. As Henry (1981: 1) notes:

> What is missing from previous accounts is the implicit and hidden contribution of informal institutions ... we need to know how these informal institutions operate, and also how they relate to their formal counterparts ... Although informal institutions and practices are, and have always been, shared and expected by people who are involved in formal institutions, they rarely feature in sociological, economic or political accounts and theorising.

I am proposing an alternative and complementary approach, that of studying society – and for that matter the American city – from the angle of informal practices. The strategy that I pursue here is 'to demarcate the informal sector as a distinct analytical and empirical category' (Papola, 1981: 13). In this rationale, I do not study informality from the standpoint of the formal system, but instead understand the formal system from the standpoint of informality. In doing so, I recognize both the centrality and

1

peripherality of informal practices and institutions in the make-up, social organization and smooth functioning of the American city at the end of the twentieth century.

It is my view that informality permeates every aspect of the functioning of society.[1] It is a vast realm – a multiplicity of niches – where human beings place themselves, either prior to the advent of an imposed formal system or within the nooks and crannies of the formal societal system. They do so in order to deal effectively with the routine issues of everyday life. Informality is understood here as a reality not totally separated from the formal system, but rather linked to and shaped by it. Informality is a structure of action that contains both harmonious (adaptation) and contradictory (resistance) relationships. It is a site of power in relation to external disciplinary and control power.

In this vein one may argue that informality 'is a point of resistance not so much against a certain class or group but against forms of power which deny the individuality of the subject. It is a site of struggle over competencies, knowledges and privileges' (Matthews, 1988: 19). Its meanings can be constructed in terms of both its genealogy and its relations to the contextual condition of the formal system.

Informality has been variously conceptualized by social scientists, depending on whether it is conceived of as a separate reality or as part of formality. It is worth presenting and analyzing briefly models of informality that have been constructed in the extant sociological and anthropological literature. Some of these can be seen as complementary in a unified theory of informality. Let us now start deconstructing in a succinct manner their basic content.

The informal system is sometimes conceived of as an alternative system. This implies that it is a separate reality. As Fitzpatrick (1988: 179) puts it, it is seen as 'essentially alternative and resistant to formal systems and, usually, as operating in diminution of them'. Criticizing the literature on informal organizations, Carlson (1958: 367) notes that 'it creates a mental image of two separate and distinct organizations in purposive organizations. It sets up mental categories of formal and informal organization and implies that all observations must be sifted into one or the other category.' This model proposes the idea that the informal system is in a state of competition, thereby attracting individual actors from the formal system to its camp with the possibility of outranking the formal system altogether. This structure of competition leads to the belief that the success of one means necessarily the failure of the other. This view of informality as forming a parallel system further leads to the notion of vertical informality (whereby the informal system can potentially hold the same kind of strength as the formal system) and horizontal informality (whereby the informal system is weaker than the formal system). As a separate reality it can be either visible or hidden – as an example, consider the underground economy.

Those who extol the dualist nature of the urban economy divide it into two systems: upper and lower circuits, traditional and modern, factory and non-factory, capitalist and subsistence. They use the organization of production as a major criterion for this distinction (Mittar, 1988: 12–13). In his study of the informal sector, Hart (1973) was among the first social scientists to observe that many income-generating activities take place in the informal sector. He proposed that to understand the mechanisms of unemployment in urban Africa, a focus on informal income opportunities would be in order.

For Harding and Jenkins (1989: 51), 'informality and formality ... should be regarded as representing the poles of a continuum'. Clearly informality is postulated here as being part of the whole; therefore it is believed to be linked to the formal system. This linkage is effected not through the core of both poles, but rather through their peripheries. The peripheries become then the point of meeting and departure of both poles. It has been empirically substantiated and argued by Papola (1981: 112) that 'the continuity of variables and submerging of one sector into another at the margin cannot be ruled out'. This corroborates an earlier observation made by Dalton (1959: 222) in his study of formal organizations. He noted that 'exclusive reliance on this couplet ignores the whole confused middle ground where there are "mixtures" and where new formal and informal actions are obscurely initiated ...when used as the counter pole of a couplet there is difficulty in saying where the informal ends and the formal begins.' One stresses here the idea that whatever differences the formal and informal may have in their core, these differences are likely to be less pronounced at the periphery, where they may even fuse. Informality becomes an extension of, even when it is in opposition to, the formal system. In this sense, one may see 'the informal and formal institutions as complementary parts of a whole' (Henry, 1981: 3).

Informality has also been conceptualized as an enclave of the formal system. It is seen as 'contained or incorporated within state power or as providing a subordinated vehicle for its expansion' (Fitzpatrick, 1988: 180). The literature on informal organizations within formal ones attests to this way of thinking. The enclave status means three different things: it is part of the formal system, it is produced by the formal system and it occupies a dependent structural position in the formal system. Its reproduction depends on the ability of the total system to reproduce the asymmetric relations between the formal and the informal system. As an enclave, it may go through a period of expansion when the formal system constricts itself or through a period of contraction when the formal system expands itself. For French economist Sauvy (1984: 131), the informal system constitutes 'islands of clandestinity' within the formal system. In this light, the informal system is seen as either related or unrelated enclaves in the formal system. The relations from one enclave to another can be either direct or indirect through the mediation of the formal system.

The 'sociology of everyday life' tends to take a different view of informality (Comeau, 1987: 115–23). In contrast with the previous model, this perspective sees the formal system as an enclave of the informal.[2] Here the informal system is believed to be as important as – or more important than – the formal (De Certeau, 1984; Maffesoli, 1989). Some propose that this is the case in some third-world countries and in specific aspects of neighborhood life in minority ethnic communities in the United States (De Soto, 1990). The formal system is literally swamped by the informal system.

Informality is also conceived of as a marginal system. The notion of marginality must be understood in its etymological meaning, that is 'at the margins of' a system. It is internal, not external. It is part of the total system. This marginality is differentiated into two categories. 'Horizontal marginality' refers to that segment *at the bottom of society* that embodies informal institutions. In this view of things, informality is the way of life of the poor. 'Vertical marginality' refers to individuals *of any social class* who locate themselves, through the use of informal ways, on the fringes of society.

Informality is also conceptualized as a parasitic system. This view is put forward mostly by government officials, social services providers and economists interested in seeing the state collecting more taxes from transactions carried out in the underground economy.[3] In this view, informality plays basically a negative role while impinging on the formal system (Tanzi, 1982). As a parasitic system it can be both external and internal, that is produced by the system. Whether its origin is inside or outside the formal system, its main action is seen to be sucking the life-blood of the formal system.

When informality is conceived of as an interstitial system, it is seen as central, that is as a glue that unites various parts of the formal system together. Graeme Shankland noted that 'it operates rather in the interstices of the formal institutions of modern urban society' (cited in Henry, 1983: 3). It does not have complete autonomy but its existence is based on its role of linking two formal units together. In that view of things, whenever there is a formal system, the informal system will strive to maintain it as a whole. It is especially in the research literature on formal organizations by both sociologists and political scientists that this vision of the informal system is expounded. For example, Chisholm (1989: 37) notes that 'the informal organization exists in the interstices between organizations'. It is seen both as making smooth the functioning of formal organizations and as a coordinating mechanism between them.

In legal studies, informality has come to mean three different processes (Matthews, 1988; Auerback, 1983; Abel, 1982). First, it refers to the transition from folk practices to a formal legal system: some folk practices have become part of the body of accepted law. Second, it covers informal aspects of formal legal practices: this is the use of informal means to achieve formal goals. And third, it refers to the informal court system whereby conflicts are solved at the family or neighborhood level – or in any case by informal means, not the formal legal system (Kolb and Bartunek, 1992).

One of the problems I confronted in explaining the nature of informality and the functioning of informal systems is defining this reality. What is the informal system? How should it be defined, so that we can study its inner working and relations to the formal system?

A formal definition of informality must take into consideration a large number of variables. These include: its origin, either as preceding the formal system or as growing from it; its relation to the formal system; the participation of its actors in the formal system; time and space factors; the meanings of everyday practices; and the structural location of informal practices in relation to other practices. Does the informal share characteristics with the formal system? These are criteria that may provide clues for a definition of the informal system.

What is informal? Informality refers to the behaviour of actors. It refers to procedures, or the outcomes of processes, whether the actors are formal or informal. Often formal institutions are linked to each other through individuals whose behaviours constitute an informal coordinating mechanism. An example is the linkage of various transport systems in the San Francisco-Oakland Metropolitan Area. Gross (1964: 59) denies the informal actor any consciousness of his or her action. He notes that 'the difference between formal and informal organizations is that while the former is a system of consciously coordinated activities, the latter is unconscious, indefinite, and rather structureless.' Dalton takes an opposite view, which is in my judgment more accurate. He notes that 'for our aim of stressing the ties between formal and informal we need to consider more than what supplies a potential for joint activity; we must talk of the activity itself. This largely conscious action is what we primarily mean by "informal"' (Dalton, 1959: 223).

The informality of any given behavior can be imputed in two ways, either through the intentionality of the actor, or through the external construction of 'informality' by the audience. In other words, one may decide to display an informal behavior or one's behavior can be defined as informal by others. The formal legal system is, ironically, what allows us in some instances to distinguish between the formal and the informal. In that vein,

Boer (1990: 405) judiciously notes that 'some activities are informal because there do not exist rules that would formalize them; other activities are informal, precisely because there are rules that either make conditions or even prohibit the activities involved. '

I define informality as a structure of action. This minimum definition implies the existence of: a place (home, street, business) where the action is carried out; actors, whose action can be either formal or informal; a formal system that informalizes the informal system; and an implicit or explicit intentionality that has a specific goal (relaxing, evading tax, political ends).

One must also recognize that there are degrees of informality. These range from very informal to almost formal. In a multi-ethnic urban environment, one identifies levels of informality in relation to the formality of the mainstream and of the minority communities. I am referring here to practices that are considered informal by minority standards. Here again, the degree of informality can be defined by internal or external criteria. The degree of an action's informality can be measured in terms of its closeness or distance from the formal system, as interpreted by the knowing subject. The closer it is to the formal system the more formal it is; the more distant, the more informal it is. Closeness and distance are not to be understood in geographical terms, but rather in a structural and hermeneutical sense. The degree of 'closeness' may be one way to compare the behavior and position of informal organizations *vis-à-vis* the formal system. As Henry (1981: 6) puts it 'rather than differentiate between informal institutions on the basis of the kinds of rules which govern the transactions and relationships within them, we can distinguish between them according to the degree to which they are integral to, or an alternative to, official institutions, and also according to their status.'

Informality shows itself in different domains. Wherever there is a density of formality, there is also a potential for informality. To be informal is human. One may go a bit further and say that behind every formal organization there is an informal institution. The multiple relations between the formal and the informal are, however, yet to be spelled out.

INFORMALITY AS A WAY OF LIFE, AS A SECTOR AND AS A SYSTEM

An analysis of informal urban practices confronts us with the need to study the everyday life of those urbanites to contribute to a general theory of practice. Human life is recognized as having both a formal and an informal side. At the individual level, informality is understood here as a way of life. At the personal level, it is a reflection of human freedom, an implicit or explicit choice that an individual actor makes to locate himself or herself in a retreat position *vis-à-vis* the formal apparatus of society. The causes for such a retreat are multiple. They include the necessity to meet a personal need, to experience a different reality, to challenge the formal system or simply to express one's socialization and one's routine of everyday life.

At the group level, informality responds to the desire of individuals to band together to accomplish stated goals without formal restrictions. It sustains the group spirit of solidarity. It plays a catalytic role in meeting the expectations of the members of the group. It allows much flexibility for the composition, decomposition and recomposition of the group.

At the institutional level, informality forms the lifeblood of formal organizations. It protects individual interests, provides an alternative experience to management and staff, restricts the control of power-holders, upgrades the influence of subaltern staff (informal leaders) and glues the corporation together. In other words, informality helps shape everyday practices and the contours of the formal system.

Informality is also seen by some researchers as a sector: economists and health care professionals use the phrase 'informal sector' of the economy or of health care. As a sector, it is understood as sharing commonalities with, and shaping the organization of a specific field, activity or domain in society. It is seen as an extension opposite or complementary to a 'formal' sector.

The notion of informality as a system implies the idea that informal practices are linked – in their individual, group and institutional dimensions – to various domains in society and share a subjugated status in terms of their relations to the formal system. The use of the concept 'system' recognizes the hierarchy of positions and differences of practices within the informal arena, but also stresses the structural links between the informal and formal systems. While the informal system is linked to the formal, it is not evident that all the sectors of the informal system are directly linked to each other. Sometimes they are so linked indirectly, through the mediation of the formal system. All the informal practices and institutions are seen as forming a system *because they display the common identity of subjugated practices.* They occupy a different structural position *vis-à-vis* the formal practices of the formal system.

THE LIMITS OF FORMALITY

We have learned from the sociology of everyday life that social existence is not made up of only formal practices. Furthermore, even these are influenced by informal practices. The rational society that the modernists have attempted to construct has not been able to formalize all of its institutions (Cook et al., 1990). Even the legal system has limits on its ability to distinguish between formal and informal practices. This is so for at least two reasons. First, the legal system does not cover every human activity. Second, legal norms do not necessarily coincide with social ones (Rose, 1983: 12). Many social practices are covered under social norms and not legal ones. They constitute parts of the realm or niches where informality flourishes.

The main problem we confront in our analysis is to explain the minutiae of the distinction between on the one hand the domain of practice which has historically differentiated through legislation and other means a formal system that is supposed to be the bedrock on which society functions and the informal system which is viewed as occupying a subordinate position, and on the other hand the 'domain of objective reality' which is made up of multiple sectors that are intertwined and feed each other. From this point of view, all sectors contribute in their own way to the overall make-up of society.

Interestingly, informality is crucial to the formal organization of modern society. For example, one sees limits to formality in the organization of the modern industrial firm. Informality pops up even in the selection and recruitment process of new employees. People are not recruited on the basis of formal tests and criteria alone – these are only part of the process. Informal means are also used to complete it. These informal means spring out of the expectation of the recruiter who is aware of the existence of informal organizations in the corporation and must assess the ability of the newcomer to meet the expectations of both the formal and informal sectors in the firm. In other words, recruiters use not only formal selection procedures, but also what Dalton (1959: 198) once called 'informal standards of fitness'.

This use of informal standards indicates that formal standards are limited in what they can do to help achieve the stated goals of the firm. Formal standards must be backed up by informal standards. One can push the argument further by stating that formal organizations are not run exclusively on the basis of formality. Since they function on the basis of both formality and informality one would naturally expect recruitment to be regulated through formal and informal means as well. The formal test or interview relies on objective criteria such as professional competence, including work experience. It refers to the technical aspect of the work. The informal test is subjective and refers to human quality and to the ability of the individual to merge with existing informal organizations, to serve as a buffer or a counterforce to informal cliques, and to be able to function as a productive element in the firm. The need for such skills may vary from one situation to another and these informal skills cannot be measured exclusively through formal tests.

The limits of formality become apparent when we try to explain the genealogy of social action, which is often a mix of both formality and informality. The informal aspects of social action are seldom taken into consideration when we study the history of urban institutions. They are the 'gray areas' and are considered rather impalpable. This has created a major problem in urban historiography, because (1) it is not always possible to trace the informal aspects of social action, (2) the result of social action is a global product consisting of the elements of both formality and informality, and (3) social action is understood as if informality did not matter much.

Examination of certain forms of social action reveals within them many informal aspects. The fact that these are subsumed under the formal aspects does not imply that they are unimportant or non-existent. It is simply a fact that we see social action as being driven by its formal aspects.

This issue of formality subsuming informality in its own expression points to the hidden nature of informality in the overall packaging of formality. This packaging leads only to a partial understanding of social action to the extent that it blurs the influence of the informal aspects in the outcome.

A central problem that needs to be solved is how we account for the contribution of informality in our formal discourse about the city. Perhaps we should begin to pay more attention to the multiple ways informality insinuates itself into formal systems. This will not solve our problem completely, but it will contribute to a better understanding of the city. We must use not only the formal angle to understand informality, but also the informal angle to understand formality.

THE SOCIAL CONSTRUCTION OF INFORMALITY

Informality is socially constructed, as is formality. Informality is a pattern of behavior that the formal system defines as being somewhat different from its own ways. The formal system has the power to define the arena of informality because it can delimit its *own* boundaries. The informal system also may seem to produce its own definition of itself as being different from the formal sector. In fact, though, the informal system does not produce a definition of informality. It either accepts or resists the rules of the formal system. It adapts itself to them.

Informality is not a property inherent in the informal system because the same institution can be declared legal or illegal, formal or informal. Informality is a *social* construction. This is why the changing legal definition of formality leads necessarily to the shifting boundaries of informality. Informality is a matter of convention (see also Herzfeld, 1988). Sometimes its boundaries are fixed by law, which can change over time.

Informality, because of its relations to formality, does not have any fixed structure – its structure shifts and may vary according to the size of the informal institution (number of people involved), its duration (period during which it functions), its location (the space it occupies) and its structural position (in a specific formal organization or in society at large).

The social construction of informality does not rest simply on the notion of legality. An informal institution or practice can be legal, not legal, illegal or criminal. An informal organization can be perfectly legal, like the clique in a formal organization. Selling a few fruits from one's garden may not be legal, but it is not illegal in the sense that there is no legal provision that prevents us from so doing, though that behavior may become criminal if we do not pay tax on this specific earning. There is no empirical basis for an *essentialist* definition of informality. Informality can be constructed only in relation to formality.

Within the informal system there are degrees of informality. A system can be informal not only in relation to the formal system but also in relation to another informal system. A distinction must be made between the informal system within the mainstream culture and that within a subculture. A behavior can be considered informal by both the formal and the informal systems, falling then into the domain of *sub-informality*. This phenomenon of sub-informality is also a social construction of reality as it owes its existence to its relation to the accepted practices of the formal system.

STRUCTURAL ORIGINS OF INFORMALITY

There must be a point at which both formality and informality emerge. This we refer to as the structural roots or origins of informality. It consists of three processes: a beginning, a separation and a relation. The beginning refers more precisely to the birth of the system, the separation to different domains in the same total system and the relation implies that formality and informality feed each other and shape each other's boundaries.

Structurally speaking informality comes about in three different ways: as a historical precedent, as a legal superimposition and as a functional adaptation. From the perspective of history, the informal system originated before the formal system. Before the advent of writing and the formal state, there existed institutions which today we refer to as informal. With the creation of the nation-state, some aspects of these existing informal organizations were co-opted and formalized. In this line of argument, the informal existed when the formal system began to be structured, and so the formal system contains an informal content that has been formalized.

In the same way that informality has historically preceded formality, in everyday life informality frequently precedes formality. We tend naturally to be informal and we use our formal cloak to interact with others and to transact formal business matters. To put it in another way, one may say that 'informal organization gives rise to formal organizations' (Barnard, 1958: 123). Because informal practices often precede formal practices, they give us clues concerning the forms formal practices would take as a result of the formalization of informal practices.

The informal system also emerges because of the superimposition of the formal system. During the colonial era, the colonists imposed on the natives a new legal system, thereby making the natives' legal system 'informal'. According to Wallerstein (1976: 58) the superimposition of the capitalist mode of production has caused the traditional mode of production – because of its newly created link with the formal colonial system – to function as an informal system.

The informal system can also be seen as an adaptation to the formalism that is superimposed. Harding and Jenkins (1989: 15) observe that 'history may be viewed as the progressive encroachment of formality upon widening areas of social life, as a consequence of literacy and the introduction of ever more sophisticated information technology, on the one hand, and the increasing power and bureaucratization of the state, on the other.'

The colonial experiment converted native institutions into informal ones, subjugated institutions whose existence was now tied to the formal institutions of the colony, and later the state. Here we see the idea that an informal institution is defined as such, not by the natives, but by the conquering power. Informality emerges here through an act of aggression and marginalization.

From a legal standpoint, informality is defined by law. The state apparatus provides a legal framework within which individuals and institutions can operate. Since the state cannot provide a legal framework for every aspect of human behavior, it becomes obvious that there is much room for the flourishing of informal practices.

Functionalists see the informal system as an outgrowth or production of the formal system. For Davies (1978: 20), 'decision-making and policies related to the formal sector define the boundaries of the informal sector. Official attitudes and legislation are crucial in determining the nature of informal activities.' The state's policies of exclusion can be a sure way for the informal system to emerge. Drug trafficking is a good example. Since it is not allowed on the open market, it goes underground. For French economist Alfred Sauvy (1984: 213), it was the simultaneous progress of industry and social legislation that led to marginal and informal economic practices.

There are now available several studies arguing and showing that the formal system gives birth to the informal system. As Boer (1990: 406) puts it, 'formalization engenders informalization'. Barnard (1958: 123), in his influential study on organization theory, concludes in the same vein in noting that 'formal organizations, once established, in their turn also create informal organizations.' For a number of researchers, the existence of the informal system cannot be explained outside that of the formal system. The existence of the formal system is a necessary requirement for the existence of the informal system.

From this perspective, the informal system emerges from the inflexibility of the formal system. To the extent that one is unable to operate an institution according to the rules of the formal system, one finds oneself located in the informal system. In other words, anything that cannot be done within the rigid structure of the formal system is likely to fall into the realm of the informal system.

The informal system emerges to fill a need because of a failure of the formal system. It helps smooth the functioning of the formal system. Its existence rests on the inability of the formal system to meet everyone's expectations. The need is created in the formal system, its fulfillment is achieved in the informal system. To the extent that the informal system provides solutions to unmet needs, it paradoxically allows participants the opportunity to continue to function in the formal system.

One must make a distinction here between permanent and sporadic failures of the formal system. In his study of the San Francisco Bay Area transport system, Chisholm (1989: 32) has observed that 'informalities may also be developed because of "episodic" failures of formal organizations that interfere with the performance of important ends ... informal channels, which tend to cut through layers of authority and provide direct contact between relevant parties, are often effective remedies.'

Since the formal system can help generate informality through its failure to satisfy all the needs of the urban citizenry, it is likely that the birth of informal practices in the American city scene cannot be relegated solely to the colonial period. Through the history of the American city, new types of informal practices have emerged in response to processes that occurred in the formal system. Thus, Sauvy (1984: 213) has identified one aspect of the birth of the informal economic system with the simultaneous progress of both social legislation and industry coupled with pressure coming from organized labor. Also, Castells and Portes (1989: 27) have linked its expansion with the process of economic restructuring of the 1970s.

THE GENEALOGICAL ORDER OF INFORMALITY

The analysis of the genealogy of informal urban practices takes us from the question of their origins to that of their history through time. We tend to think of the origins as before the advent of western formality, or as produced by it. The colonization of native institutions accounts for the former, while the inability of the formal system to regulate every aspect of life explains the latter.

Western formality was the ideological apparatus that sustained colonization and is one form of experimentation in the ordering of society from the European viewpoint. It is basically a way of unifying the world through a system of logic that western rationality can understand and of course manipulate. In the United

States, the establishment of the formal system has led to the production of minority communities. The informalization of minority institutions has a different political meaning than that found among the mainstreamers. In the minority communities, informality was produced through an *act of aggression* and the forced subjugation of the people. In the mainstream community, formality came about as the result of the *victory of reason over traditions*. Thus, the informalization process consisted in the imposition and upgrading of the rational western formal system and the downgrading of folk and minority ways.

There are two types of historical continuity involved here in our analysis of the genealogy of informality. The evolution of informality that precedes formality takes various shapes. The informal system remains a site of counterpower and functions within the framework of the formal system and is shaped by it. The informal system may be co-opted by the formal system and be under its control. It may either coalesce or maintain its identity. However, the informal system can adopt a retreat position until the time comes when its practices can be revitalized and resurface under better circumstances.

The genealogy of subjugated practices has a different dynamic because of the influence from the dominant sector that it must adjust to. The informal system must adjust its ways to constraints generated by the formal system for its survival, adaptation and expansion. I agree with Davies (1978: 20–1) when he notes that 'the informal sector is both dependent on and peripheral to the formal sector. It develops in spite of restrictions but the extent and nature of that development are invariably subject to those restrictions.'

The genealogy of informality when it is produced by formality tends to evolve according to people's needs and the formal circumstance that give it birth. For example, there are informal practices that are instantaneous or have a one-purpose orientation. When the goal is met, the informal system may cease to survive. These are informal practices that either coalesce with the formal system or give birth to other forms.

The genealogy of informality must be understood in three different ways: (1) the genealogy of the formation of the informal system, (2) the genealogy of the informal system once it is established, and (3) the genealogy of the relations between the formal and informal system. One may refer to the first as *formative* or *constitutive* genealogy, to the second as *developmental* or *evolutionary* genealogy, and to the third as *associative* or *relational* genealogy.

Constitutive genealogy concentrates on the various units, the relations between them and the behavioral, symbolic and ideological content of the informal system. It deconstructs the informal system as a way of unveiling the multiple patterns that may lead to its reconstitution.

Developmental genealogy concentrates on the transmutation of the informal system. This includes the history of hidden structures that reappear in the make-up of the informal system. It analyses the behavior of both informal systems co-opted by the formal system, and folk institutions like ethno-medicine that continue to survive side by side with the formal system. The informal may be formed to respond to a specific problem. Once the problem is solved or diminished, the informal system may move to a latent state to be activated later for the same or a similar purpose. As Chisholm (1989: 67) observes, when 'the formal channel works well enough ... the informal channel stays mostly dormant. It is not usually needed but remains available.'

Some informal practices remain dormant after a formal system has been established – dormant, not eliminated, because they reappear cyclically in the interstices of the formal system. Their expressions continue to take the same shape and have the same meanings. When the formal system goes through a crisis, it may be unable to contain them in their hidden niches. Hence informal practices sometimes reappear at the moment when the formal system is in a state of crisis. Foucault (1980: 6) speaks of informal practices 'which predate the setting up of a judicial system and which are regularly revived in popular uprisings'. The genealogy of these practices has four main features: (1) their appearance is cyclical; (2) they depend on the breakdown of the formal system; (3) they remain in a state of dormancy in between crises in the formal system; and (4) their genealogy is pretty much tied up with that of the formal system.

The genealogy of the informal system cannot be understood outside the framework of the genealogy of the formal system because the latter constantly produces, influences or allows the recognition of the existence of new informalities. Because their genealogical development is linked to that of the formal system, we refer to this as *associative genealogy*. It is the genealogy of the relationships between the formal and informal system.

Furthermore, the informal system serves as a reservoir attracting formal practices that have been marginalized and informalized. They remain in this niche until better circumstances allow those informalized formal practices to de-informalize themselves and regain their position in the formal system.

The genealogy of informal practices may vary according to their status in a given system. They may be rejected, persecuted, made illegal or neutralized by the formal apparatus of society. The variation will be the result of the differences in the way in which they are tied to the formal system.

Associative genealogy addresses the issue of the relational imperative not only as related to the influence that one exerts on the other, but also the trajectory from informal to formal and vice versa. Concrete situations and their deconstructions provide the field of study where one can analyze the relations of one to the other, the implications of one in the other, the production of one by the other, and the failure or the success of one to reproduce the other.

'RAW' VERSUS 'COOKED' INFORMALITY

Much of what has been said so far concerns the behavior of 'raw' informality, a form of informality that is not purposefully created by the formal institutional system. Within the firm, raw informality implies both discrimination and secrecy. In the formal firm, it is an arena in which a small group or a clique can participate and in a sense discriminate against other people who are not invited to join in. Because others are barred from becoming part of the group, it tends to be secretive, in the sense that only the members are privy to the content of the information exchanged among them.

In contrast, 'cooked' informality is purposeful, planned and open to a larger group. It is cooked in the sense that it is created by and for a smooth functioning of the formal system. In the modern firm, it refers to informal gathering where the dress code is 'down' and people are called to behave informally. This cooked informality is meant to break down class, ethnic and gender barriers and to transform the members of the corporation into the members of an informal family.

Informality is cooked to better serve the interests of the corporation, to allow the members to know each other better, to root the group informally in the corporation, to iron out difficulties created in the formal system and to express the human side of the corporation. Because it is cooked by the formal system, one may say it constitutes a formalized form of informality.

THE PERIPHERALITY OF THE INFORMAL SYSTEM

A system cannot be peripheral in itself. Peripherality is not a matter of essence, but rather of existence, that is of relationship. Something can be peripheral only in relation to a core or central system. The fact that a system is formal does not mean that it is a central system. There are formal systems that are peripheral in relation to other formal systems. The fact that a system is informal means necessarily that it is peripheral. Yet, it can be central in relation to other satellite or peripheral systems.

One may wonder why the informal system is a peripheral one. It is so only when we look at its relationship with formal institutions through which it can be further peripheralized or come closer to the formal system. One may conclude that the formal system peripheralizes the informal system so that it may accomplish the following three things: (1) it may expand its basis of operation as a way of reducing the sphere of activity of the informal system; (2) it may dominate the informal system so as to be able to control its arena with a view to making it dependent on the formal system; and (3) it may trivialize and neutralize the informal system in order to eliminate it.

The informal system is peripheral because of the existence of a center in the formal system. The informal is judged according to the mainstream values and behaviors of those attached to the center. The center sets the standards. The farther away a system is from the standards of the center the more peripheral it is. The informal system is evaluated, appreciated or stigmatized according to the logic of the mainstream formal system.

The informal system is peripheral by reason of its structural location in relation to the formal system. The people who participate in the informal system behave according to the rule of the system. Peripherality must be understood in structural terms and not simply in terms of geographic space. Structurally speaking, it is not located at the core of the formal system.

The informal system is peripheral because the formal system assigns it such a status. The peripherality of its informality comes about because it is recognized and labeled as such by the formal system or simply because it is rejected by the formal system. It is peripheral not necessarily because there is something inherent in it that is false, immoral or criminal, but simply because it fails to get a formal recognition from the formal system.

The informal system is peripheral because of the kinds of activities in which people are involved. All human activities are by definition human so they cannot be informal because they are not human. These are human activities that are not considered formal by the formal system and this factor tends to reinforce their informal character. They may become illegal which means that to survive the actors must go underground or use illegal means.

The informal system is peripheral because of the rationale used that may be different from that used in the mainstream formal system. It can be both the reason for the rejection of the informal system and the reason for its stability – because it follows its own logic.

The informal system is peripheral because of the intentionality of the actors. Although they may participate full time in the formal system, they may also participate in the informal system. They, themselves, make a distinction and adjust their behaviors as they move from the formal to the informal system. This is a subjective criterion they use to identify the peripheral character of the informal system. The actors recognize that their action belongs to a domain different from that of the formal system.

The informal system is peripheral because its actors may be powerless and in no position to force the formal recognition of the informal system. This lack of power is what defines the status of the informal system. It is also what makes possible its control by the formal system.

What is the structure of the peripherality of the informal system? Because the informal system is peripheral, it comprises both a core and a periphery. We must then study the informal system both in its internal make-up and its external linkage.

The core of the informal system is able to expand itself by constricting the periphery. The core maintains itself because it is the incarnation of power and the mainstream standards. The periphery can also expand itself at the expense of the core. Both can expand their boundaries through co-optation and invasion.

Periphery may be discussed in relation to both the central mainstream system and the core of the informal system. The periphery of the informal system is closer to the core of the informal system than to the core of the mainstream system. The core in the informal system has a status similar to the periphery in the mainstream system *vis-à-vis* the center in the mainstream system. Both are peripheral to the mainstream core.

The relationship between the center and the periphery in the formal system does not operate necessarily in the same way as that between the center and the periphery in the informal system. In a multi-ethnic urban environment, one would expect the center and periphery in a minority community to be influenced and shaped by a sub-cultural orientation that may be different from the dominant mainstream culture.

By deconstructing the relations between the core and the periphery, one unmasks a set of relationships. These include: the relation of the formal system to the informal in the mainstream; the relation of the core of the informal system to the periphery in the informal system; and the relations of the formal to the informal system.

The informal system in its relation to the formal system may achieve a certain level of stability or routinization. In this kind of environment, total co-optation of the informal by the formal system could lead to total integration. Total co-optation of the formal by the informal system could lead to a complete reversal of societal ways because the informal would necessarily become the formal. Partial co-optation by the informal system is likely to lead to polarization because of the strengthening of the informal system. Partial co-optation by the formal system necessarily leads to more integration.

INFORMALITY AND URBAN PRACTICES

As paradoxical it may sound, the informal system is also central. The centrality of informality becomes manifest when the societal system is studied from the angle of informality. The emphasis and focus on the informal angle is privileged here so as to better understand social action in its everyday practices (see also Bourdieu, 1990). The sociology of everyday life provides the two necessary tools needed to achieve this end.

The focus on everyday life allows us a different perspective than that of private sphere versus public life one finds so vigorously debated in the feminist literature (Nicholson, 1990; Rosaldo, 1974; and Moore, 1988). It is not empirically sound to locate the informal exclusively in the domain of private life. While one does not deny its existence there, or the importance of private life as the arena where the informal is consolidated and where the strategies for informal action are often plotted out before an informal behavior can be implemented in the public life, the informal has always been well alive in the public sphere.

In the previous section, we have discussed how from the standpoint of the formal system the informal system is seen as peripheral and secondary. In this section we will discuss how, in a bottom-up approach to the city, the informal system must also be viewed as playing a central role. It is so because the formal system operates on the basis of both formal and informal rules.

The centrality of informality stems from the empirical observation that it is located foremost in the individual actor, who is the human agent in whom we find a mixture of informal and formal behavior and practices. Even when we are studying the behavior of a specific structure or organization, we can not afford to dismiss the control of the human agent.

The informal is central because it is the locus of private life. Here the individual recoups his or her strengths, plots out strategies and regains his or her freedom away from the constraints of public life, whether generated by government or business. One

cannot understand what sustains public life or public bureaucracies if the informal life of its agents is left untouched.

The centrality of informality remains in the fact that some of
its aspects predate formality and some others are produced
by formality. In any case, the formal system depends on it, is
shaped by it, and attempts to transform it and possibly to colonize it.
De Certeau (1984) sees informality in everyday life as it insinuates itself through ruse and tactics into the formal system.

The informal life, to the extent that it provides a layout for the
expression of freedom and produces a subterranean form of
socialite through a manifestation of human solidarity, is central to
the production of the formal system (Maffesoli, 1989). It is the
locus where everyday life manifests itself, where solutions are
sought to remedy failures in the formal system, and where
resistance is galvanized.

It is a form of power to the extent that knowledge is shared,
and back-alley strategies are developed. It provides an alternative perception of society. Within the overarching arm of formal
society, the individual pulls back to regain his or her freedom, to
create a free space, to strengthen his or her position, to undermine rivals, to consolidate his or her basis, to acquire knowledge.

The importance, hence the centrality, of informality stems from
the fact that public life is shaped by it, it grows in the nooks and
crannies of public bureaucracy, and it stands as an arena that is
used and exploited by the formal system but cannot be totally
colonized by it.

THE MEANINGS OF INFORMAL URBAN PRACTICES

An exegesis of informal urban practices recognizes the diversity
and heterogeneity of such acts. Their commonality resides in the
fact they occupy, if not a subjugated position, at least one that is
not under the direct surveillance of the formal system. There are
two basic locations for the performance of informal urban practices: the individual, and the group or the institution.

Postmodern thinking celebrates the return of the subject. The
subject is here at the very heart of our distinction, in the sense
that he or she decides or not to engage in informal practices.

Urban informality is the expression of the freedom of the subject. This means freedom from the constraints of formal institutional life, but also freedom as a kind of manifest destiny where the self affirms itself. The yearning for human freedom cannot be controlled or contained by the regulations or conventions of formal society. Informal practices provide a corridor for the protection of the self against regulatory structures.

Informal urban practices also mean that the hidden structure they provide is a resilient but fundamental aspect of the make-up of society. These practices are made possible within a web of relationships. Through this we can identify the relational as the second characteristic of informal urban practices. This aspect is expressed through human solidarity in terms, for example, of gift and exchange in general. This characteristic is probably the more visible and better known, perhaps because of the works of Marcel Mauss on the notion of gift, but also because in everyday life we can pinpoint instances where people help each other in informal ways.

Informal urban practices finally mean that the hidden structure they provide is also one of resistance, both passive and active. Whichever way, such a structure of resistance must be seen as being either anti-formal system or complementary to the formal system. The idea of resistance implies the recognition of the resiliency of cultural traditions that cannot easily be brushed aside by the formal system.

THE LOGIC OF THE 'INFORMAL CITY' APPROACH

Our argument is that there exists an informal city located just beneath and in the interstices of the formal city. The metaphor is not geographical, but rather structural and hermeneutical. This is the city where maneuvers that cannot be done publicly, legally, ethically or otherwise are performed. This is the resilient cultural arena that supports, or sometimes obstructs, but is always in interaction with the formal system.

Why is it important to study or pay attention to the informal side of the city, since in many cases these structures are hidden? There are several reasons. At the outset, one may advance that the occurrence of informal practices has always been known simply because we participate in them, even though we tend to consider them unimportant. After all, positivist thinkers such as Karl Marx, Max Weber and Emile Durkheim have not made informality the center of their intellectual preoccupation.

Our approach is to question the positivist thinking about hierarchy. In this tradition, the hierarchical and formal is considered more important than the informal. They are not seen as interdependent systems which share a common reality and feed each other's existence.

Our approach recognizes the importance of informal practices as providing a balance to formal practices. It is a 'bottom-up' approach in the sense that it magnifies or makes visible informal reality so as to show its dialectical relations with the formal system. It stresses that its existence must be acknowledged if we are to comprehend the societal system and make useful urban policies.

Because informality is the other side of formality, it is considered to be one instance of a mechanism of power. It is used by the formal system to strengthen its power. It is used by the informal system in the same way as well to infiltrate or challenge formal power.

The informal city is seen as omnipresent in the nooks and crannies of the city. It is found in informalization of urban space, the informal economy, informal policy in judicial systems, the clique system in the modern firm and informal communication in public bureaucracies. And, it is found, of course, in neighborhoods and family practices. In a sense, it is a vibrant city. An analysis of its parameters, its operation and relation to the formal system is a necessary step toward understanding urban process.

My interest in attempting to conceptualize the structure of informality comes from a general observation of the American city scene. Put very simply, it is my view that informal practices – which are by no means trivial – constitute an important factor in the shaping of everyday life at the personal, group and institutional levels. In fact, these informal practices shape, sustain, support, undermine and influence in many different ways the flow of processes and activities of the formal system of society. Without them, the formal system would not be able to function

The Informal City

smoothly. They constitute an integral part of its operation. The informal city is seen then as the *hidden dimension* of the formal city. In this light, I am proposing that the study of informality be used as an alternative and complementary route for the understanding of the formal apparatus of the American city.

Notes

1. The informal aspect of societal life remains constant. There is, however, a variability in the manifestation of the phenomenon. It can be household, workplace or social-function based.
2. For a critical review of the literature on the sociology of everyday life, see Comeau (1987).
3. This phenomenon has also its political and social ramifications. If the informals do not pay taxes, it is argued that the city and the state may not have the necessary resources to provide basic services to the local urban community. Furthermore, informals are seen as individualists who do not contribute to the common good, but rather work for their personal gain.

2

Informal Space

On the American urban scene – including the San Francisco Bay Area – everyday life contains both a formal and informal dimension. Such informal practices are not trivial, but rather constitute an essential factor that helps shape the structure of the formal societal system. To further ground empirically our theory of the centrality of the relations between informality and formality in the organization of the modern American city, let us attempt to analyze the anchoring of informal practices in the organization of urban space. The informal city needs an informal territorial infrastructure to anchor its informal practices in the organization of the urban space. Such informal space exists, and provides a basis for the carrying out of these kinds of action.

Informality does not occur in a vacuum. The space where the informal practices take place is often a formal space that has been informalized. The multiplicity and variety of informal spaces cannot be ignored if we want to understand the role of informality in the American city. It becomes a central issue here, and therefore the object of our study, because of its relations to both the formal space and informal practices. It is not simply what we do that gives an informal content to the formal space, but also structural boundaries and constraints generated within the formal system.

Previously, the concept of informal space has been used mainly in the field of proxemic studies and refers to the spatial distances individuals maintain in encounter interactions with others. Hall (1966: 105), who introduced the concept of informal space in the anthropological literature, did so to identify this specific category of spatial experience. In his view, space becomes informal or is created as such 'because it is unstated, not because it lacks form or has no importance ... Informal spatial patterns have distinct bounds, and such deep, if unvoiced, significance that they form an essential part of the culture' (Hall, 1966: 105). This loose defini-

tion of informal space implies that it is a social construction and
the presence of at least two individuals and the distances maintained between them in interacting with each other are a *sine qua
non*. In this context, the notion of informal space is interchange-
able with that of personal space. Other researchers have extended
the notion of informal space to include or cover the interactions
of individuals with the physical environment of buildings. Sitton
(1980: 65–82), for example, has argued that there is a hidden
dimension in the interaction of the American student population
with public school structures and discusses the negative impact
of these structures on student behavior. He concludes that,
because of its impersonal character, the public school's spatial
arrangement negatively influences the level of interaction among
teachers, administrators and students. In a sense, he is challenging architects to build public structures that meet both the formal
and informal needs of the users (see also Sommer, 1983; Ellis
et al., 1985).

Although the encounter is important in the production of
informal or personal space, our aim will not be to discuss spatial
distances among individuals locally or cross-culturally the way
Hall did, or self-management styles, procedures and tactics following the path of the dramaturgical analyses of Erving Goffman
(1959, 1961). Rather, in this chapter, we analyze the relations
between formal and informal space, the production of informal
space, the changing spatial identity of the workplace and the
geography of urban informality. Space is a flexible entity – a
socio-political production – that can be informalized, and, in the
San Francisco Bay Area, it clearly serves as an infrastructural
basis for the performance of informal practices.

THE SOCIAL PRODUCTION OF INFORMAL SPACE

The urban landscape in the San Francisco Bay Area (as in many
other regions) is divided into formal space and informal space
where daily activities and practices are carried out. The formal
space is regulated and falls immediately under the jurisdiction of
various agencies of the state or the local government.[1] It con-
forms to city laws. This is why developers and other individuals

must seek permission in order legally to transform unoccupied into occupied land, according to laws set by the formal system.

The informal space is more elusive. Sometimes, as unregulated space, it may not be under the direct control of city government. It can either precede the establishment of formal space or be produced by formal space or the formal use of space.

Prior to the formal use of the urban space, there is an informal use of that space. Through the establishment of city codes, the formal system slowly invades the informal space and brings it into the orbit of the formal by transforming it into formal space, with the purpose of controlling it. The city government is always devising formal rules so as to reduce the extent of informal space.

Informal space is also a product of the formal use of the urban space. Because the formal system is unable to meet the expectations of every member of the city community, individuals feel it necessary to transform formal space into informal space to conduct their informal activities. Informal space develops in this instance within the formal spatial system. It is an outgrowth of that system.

There are a number of ways that specific spatial units have been informalized in the San Francisco-Oakland Metropolitan area. However, the process of informalization of this urban landscape is very different from that of the typical third-world city. In both sites, one witnesses the transformation of the urban landscape into informal spatial units, manifested most strikingly in the informal appropriation of parcels of urban land for settlement. This is the most visible and spectacular form of spatial informalization in the third world. The land is appropriated slowly by squatters who occupy unused or vacant lots. The squatters invade the land, build their shacks, and transform the area into an informal settlement until such time as it is either bulldozed or incorporated into the formal city system.

In the case of the third-world squatter settlements, the land that was vacant is now occupied and has become informalized as a spatial entity or has gone through a process of informalization. The process of appropriation is itself informal in the sense that no officially recognized ownership of paper is signed. The property is simply taken or bought from another squatter. Even when the area has already been occupied, informality continues to creep in, in the creation of alleys, for example, and in the survival of informal architecture expressed in the squatters' houses. What makes the area an informal entity is the social use of the land that does not fall under the regulatory mechanisms of the city government.

This form of informalization of the urban space does not go on to such a degree of magnitude and visibility in the American city. The informalization of the urban space is more subtle and may not have a permanent character. Nevertheless, in the San Francisco Bay Area, public space is still informalized in several different ways for different purposes.

People informalize public and private places to conduct informal business or social transactions, or simply to meet basic human needs. This is the case of the individual merchant in Oakland who transforms his portico into a marketplace, displaying his merchandise, attracting a clientele, and engaging in informal economic transactions. It is an informal market because the owner bypasses zoning laws and uses his own property as an informal market site. The conversion of the formal space into an informal entity can occur not only outside the house, but inside the house as well. In this latter case, a portion of the house may be used as an informal shop.

The street vendor converts the area where he operates his business into an informal space. Whether it is the drug dealer who stands in a corner of an Oakland street, the seller of stolen goods who stands in front of a store on Market Street in San Francisco, or an unlicensed street vendor who operates in front of a public school in Berkeley, they all share the same characteristics in regard to the use of public space. They convert it into something informal – that is, an informal site where informal market transactions are carried out.

Public space is informalized also when it is transformed into a sleeping site by informal actors. Homeless people are seen to congregate and sleep in public parks, or in front of public buildings or privately owned stores. They transform or convert these spaces into informal ones. The sites are used for purposes different from that assigned to them by the formal societal system.

Informalization of urban space can also be seen in terms of both supply and demand. So far we have looked at the process from the supply side, as in the case of those who transform a formal space into an informal one as a way of displaying their merchandise or conducting their businesses. When seen from the demand side, the space can be informalized by individuals who are looking for suppliers. This is the case of the person who asks an informal mechanic to work or repair his car in front of his house, thereby transforming the space into an informal garage.

TIME, SPACE AND INFORMALITY

The time factor is an important element in understanding how informal space is produced and organized in relation to formal space. Informal space is the result of formal space being used for informal purposes. Informal space can have a permanent, transitional or recurrent character. A locale can be formalized quasi-permanently until such a time as it is incorporated into the formal space. The squatter settlement in the third-world city is a good example of this type. In the United States, the junk yard fulfills a similar role. It is an informal marketplace where one acquires secondhand parts for one's own car or to repair someone else's car. Informal mechanics sometimes use it in this way instead of going to an auto parts and accessories store in the formal economy.

Informal space can be a transitional space. A room in a house may be used as a shop until the owner is able to move the operation to the formal sector. It becomes a recurrent space when a public space such as part of an office is used on and off as an informal space. The water-cooler is a traditional locus of gossip in formal organizations; the place is sporadically transformed into an informal location to allow information to flow through the grapevine. Such use may be cyclical when the space is informalized at a given time on a weekly, monthly or yearly basis. It may be incidental when the space is used for a one-off informal event.

GEOGRAPHY OF THE INFORMAL SPACE

The geography of the informal space can be described in terms of the niches where informal activities take place (Whyte, 1980). The production of these informal locations is related to the kinds of informal activity that the people are engaged in. Public places like garage stations (informal mechanics), public street, (street vendors) and street corners (drug dealers) are informalized, as are private homes when politicians hold informal political meetings in constituents' houses or when an informal entrepreneur transforms a room in the home into a sweatshop. Gossipers and cliques create informal spatial niches in formal organizations. Others informalize the public space, not for the purpose of engaging in transactions with other people, but to take care of their own needs, as is the case of the homeless who use the park for sleeping at night. In every city, there are niches of converted space that become informal. Spatial informality can be characterized by way of the intentionality or personal needs of the actor, with the individual often aware of his or her unconventional action. Spatial informality occurs also by way of a transaction whereby actors from both sides expect to gain something from the interaction. Spatial informality is also produced by way of politicization whereby higher goals are anticipated for the benefit of the community.

In a study of the informal economy in New York City, informalization of space has been described in terms of the spatial location of informal economic activities. These informal locations came about because of the 'concentration of informal activities in immigrant communities ... in areas undergoing residential and commercial gentrification ... [and] the concentration of manufacturing and industrial services in certain areas that emerge as a new type of manufacturing district or service market' (Sassen-Koob, 1989: 70–2).

The geography of the informal space in the San Francisco-Oakland Metropolitan Area has its low and high densities of operation. There are three major areas where informal space can easily be identified in the city. One is entire immigrant enclaves, like the Chinatowns and the San Francisco Mission District with its Hispanic population. In these places, people freely continue to engage in practices considered informal by formal standards. The informal economy is very strong here, as the residents transact business outside the regulatory norms and rules of the formal city government. These districts also provide a spatial niche for those who run and work in sweatshops which are extensions or branches of open manufacturing businesses located in the formal space of the city. A portion of the work ostensibly produced in the open shop is actually done in the sweatshop. This kind of informal space sustains the façade of the formal operation. Here we see a contrast between the open shop and the closed shop. In the latter, all the activities, formal or informal, are carried out in the shop and not in its invisible branches.

The second, more dispersed major area where space is informalized is public places and streets, and the third is the residential home, which serves sometimes as a workplace for housekeepers, gardeners and other workers. These various niches serve in their own way as places where informal practices are carried out. This is why, when we look at the city, we find that the same places are used for different purposes and the expression of informality as a way of life has indeed a territorial basis of support. The deatomization of the urban space leads necessarily to the division between formal and informal space.

When we study the city from the angles of formality and informality, we understand that the urban landscape is also divided into a front region and a back region (Goffman, 1963, 1972; Giddens, 1984: 122–6). The front region is the locus of the formal sector and is the center of formality or the mainstream culture. The back region is identified with the periphery and is the locus of the informal sector or the center of informality. The front region occupies the center space and the back region the peripheral space. The front region uses the center of power to control, coerce, contain and discipline the back region. The back region in turn uses or develops an informal system of practices to circumvent control by the front region.

Between the front region and the back region stands the middle region where brokers, middlemen and intermediaries translate front region policies for the back region and relate back-region demands to front-region decision-makers. This middle region, according to Meyrowitz (1985: 271), produces 'behavior that lacks the extreme formality of the former front region behavior and also lacks the extreme informality of traditional back region behavior.' The notion of space is linked to that of the identity of the social system. The front region is the domain of the center, the back region the domain of the periphery and the middle region is the domain of the brokers or the political leaders.

The city can be deconstructed in terms of these three localities of informality. The front region has its informal niches in its midst, informality within the formal sector. Informality also arises in its periphery, that is the back region. To link the front to the back region, a third structure, one of mediation, is developed in the middle region, which in turn produces its own informality.

Front region and back region correspond to specific domains of power. The front region uses its network of offices and agencies to regulate the back-region people and the land they occupy. Districts and local neighborhoods may elect individuals to represent them in the front region, but the policies of the city are not back-region policies (even though they may have the same input in their formation), but they are indeed front-region policies that back-region people must conform to in their use of the land. These representatives may have one leg in the front region and the other in the back region in order to sell front-region policies to back-region residents. One sees here how the informalization of the urban space provides an infrastructural basis of support for the formal political structure in its informal manifestation.

Even within the periphery itself, or back region, we find that the space is further divided into front and back regions. Formal enterprises there may have a front and a back region. The front region is used for formal business and the back region for informal activities like, for example, the numbers game. The front region provides a cover for the operation of activities in the back region. The back region in a restaurant, where one may participate in the numbers game, attracts individuals who may be prospective clients for the front region where the legitimate business – serving food – is in full swing.

In our analysis of the informalization of urban space, we must turn to the role of the home in that process. We said earlier that space is a flexible entity that can be formalized or informalized. Space that is delimited along formal lines, such as a house, becomes objectively formalized according to the official purpose for which it is appropriated and used. The house's formal entity is as a home.

The home is itself subdivided into a front and a back region. The front region is the most formal area of the house where visitors are welcomed. The back region (back room, basement, yards) is the most informal part of the house. As applied to the home, the notion of formal and informal space may not be cut and dried. The home is a fluid domain where formality and informality coexist side by side.

Urban space can belong to someone, a corporation or the state. It becomes informalized when it is used for informal activities. One usually does not think of a home as being something formal except in matters relating to property rights. However, in everyday life, the conduct of our life is often informal, relaxed and private. It is the display of our natural and unmasked self.

Although the home is a workplace for all of us, we tend not to look at it that way for the simple reason that we seldom get paid for things done for the family. The money return for home activities is not immediate or even expected. We are more aware that it is a formal workplace when we use the home to conduct formal businesses, the kind of work we might do in an office, for example. We formalize and informalize our residence in terms of zoning. Workplace and living room (formal), versus the rest of the house (informal). One room becomes our office, that is our factory. This is where we produce work to be sold to others, while in the other rooms we may do work for the rest of the family.

What is for us a home can also be a workplace for others. One may speak of the dual vocation of the home as both a formal place – a home – and an informal place – a workplace. The poor from the inner city see the upper-class home as a workplace, that is a factory. This is a place where they can work and earn an income. It is not a place where they live, rest or eat. They come there to work as gardeners, maids or informal professionals. In their own way, they informalize these formal units of the urban landscape. One may say that the home, street, public building or place each has potentially a double identity, formal and informal.

INFORMAL SPACE AND THE ETHNIC MINORITY NEIGHBORHOOD

It seems at first that one of the characteristic features of the ethnic minority neighborhood is the widespread existence of informal practices. To a certain extent, informality gives a distinct personality to the ethnic neighborhood in contrast to the formality of the mainstream urban community.

The ethnic minority neighborhood may be defined as a locus where a community manufactures its own informal system to serve as the organizational rules of its adaptation. This system links the people together, creates a subculture of informality in interactions with the formal system of mainstream society, participates in informal ways in the formal social system, informalizes certain aspects of formal organization, and strides through routinization towards the legitimization of the informal system.

I define the ethnic minority enclave as a locus where practices labelled by the formal sector as 'informal' are produced to handle the residents' relations with the mainstream social and formal system. The social construction of the identity of the ethnic neighborhood as a spatial entity evolves and articulates itself with the mainstream system.

It is not simply by formal means that urban land is appropriated. Real estate agents play a key role in the distribution process of urban land. They have their own formal and informal ways of doing business. Informal strategies often influence formal outcome. When a real estate agent chooses to show a house in a black neighborhood to a black client, he or she is often making an informal assessment of the formal needs of the client. The process of acquisition of urban land is itself partly informalized.

THE MULTIDIMENSIONAL GEOMETRY OF THE URBAN SPACE

We cannot study urban spatial units as if they were either formal or informal. For Sack (1980: 7), 'space means the space of the physical world, and geometry is the language in which it is described.' When viewed from the perspective of time, we tend to see spatial units as having a multidimensional geometry – in contrast to the usual three-dimensional Euclidian geometry – which can be understood in terms of their changing identity, the expansion of production and the internationalization of informal practices.

Time–space compression allows us to identify the temporal distribution of informality in any given space. A single space can be formal at 8:00 a.m., become informal at 9:00, to be formalized again at 10:00 a.m. The changing identity of the formal space and its transformation into an informal space is largely dependent on informal practices carried out in such a place.

Another example is that of linking the formal identity of the space to official practices that produce informality. Formal office space is informalized on days when the office holder does not expect to interact with the public: the dress code is down, the office is used as if it were a home space to diminish stress and to allow a recovery of the self. One day the office space is formal, and the next it is informal. Such use reveals the limits of formal architecture and its inability to model place in terms of both the formal and the informal preoccupations of the individual subject. In a sense, formal architecture is coercive, disciplinary and restrictive. It forces the individual to adapt to the formal structure and, if the need arises, to informalize it. It is non-dualist in the sense that it does not provide two structures, formal and informal, that an individual could use at will. It is part of the project of rational society that architecture should discipline the body to behave formally in a formal space.

The multidimensionality of the urban space is also manifest in the expansion of production. We find in San Francisco a Chinese repairman who uses an office space that is open to the public and legal. It is where he transacts business with his clients. He receives there items to be fixed and returns them to the owner once repaired. The repair work is not done in this office, but rather in a back-region workshop located in another house in the city. This workshop is illegal: it operates without a permit, is closed to the public and is located in a private home. It is an informal operation that feeds the formal practices of the front office. We see here a clear use of the formal sector to informalize the back region, which in return supports the operation of the formal sector.

The third factor that contributes to the informalization of the landscape is the internationalization of informal practices. This is done through what I call informal diplomacy and others refer to as paradiplomacy or microdiplomacy (Duchacek, 1984; Soldatos, 1990). By informal diplomacy I mean to indicate the ability of the city or groups in the city to develop and establish their own foreign policies and diplomatic relations with a foreign country. These relations have been carried out in the past only on a national level, by appointed diplomats and through official channels. This is the role of the ambassador, the special envoy of the president or a delegation from the government. Such diplomacy handles official business between two governments. Informal diplomacy is now carried out by cities, and can undermine or strengthen the national effort. The city of Berkeley, for example, had adopted a city in Nicaragua and helped the Sandinistas in many different ways while the United States government was helping the Contras. Churches in Berkeley, Oakland and San Francisco provide sanctuaries to Nicaraguan, Guatemalan and Salvadorean refugees against official policy that considers them illegal aliens and wants to expel them from the country. Through using the church as a home, the refugees have contributed to the informalization of the urban space in a way analogous to the practice of third-world refugees from rural areas who build squatter settlements on the physical margins of the primate cities.

THE 'BLURRING OF GENRES'

The advent of information technology makes possible the informalization of the workplace and the formalization of the home. It is no longer necessary for some types of work to be done by full-time employees and in a workplace. Such classes of workers are now able to stay at home producing work on their computers for formal firms in the San Francisco Bay Area.[2] They are able to receive at home the work to be done, complete the job and return the finished product – all without having to leave home.

The shift from the home front to a central office or manufacturing plant is of recent origin and dates back to the beginning of the industrial revolution. Information technology provides us the means and allows us an opportunity to return to the home as a formal work station. Concurrently, the formal central workplace may become partly informalized in that it is now used by these homeworkers as a place to get involved in informal activities.

To explain this revolutionary trend in the workplace, Schiff (1983: 23) has coined the word 'flexiplace'. For him, 'flexiplace involves giving people greater options on where they work, including possibilities to work at home part or all of the time'. That flexibility of moving one's workplace from the formal office to the home has caused the blurring of genres and the partial meshing of informal with formal space.

There are now many firms who used the flexiplace strategy in the San Francisco Bay area to lower their overhead costs, to take advantages of an available pool of specialist laborers, and thus to get ahead of their competitors. Many workers prefer this type of arrangement because of their dislike of office work and as a way of meeting their own psychological needs (see also Lozano, 1985).

INFORMATIONAL SPACE AND INFORMALITY

With the advent of high technology, we find a different form of insinuation of informality into the spatial domain. Information technology has led to a crumbling of spatial boundaries and spatial constructions as it insinuates itself into the formal space, but it also crosses the boundaries of the formal city and for that matter of the state itself. These informational or communications spaces, which cannot be directly regulated by the state because of their multiple shapes and forms (the state may, however, try to intervene if there is any indication of potential criminal behavior), are in fact informalized spaces. For example, the telephone and computer are used to maintain and strengthen informal contacts inside and outside the city. The face-to-face interaction needed for urban relational informal practices before the advent of information technology is no longer so essential. Such interactions now go on through the mechanisms of what Castells calls the 'space of flows'.

These new informal spatial forms are the locus of a hidden power. They are reproduced and administered through informal means, and because they are fluid and cannot be controlled totally by formal power, they have the potential either to strengthen or undermine the regulatory mechanisms of formal power. Behind the computers, groups related through informal networks of communication hold power and influence the formal flow of the formal system.

Information technology inserts the 'space of flows' into the 'space of places'. Castells (1989: 6) notes that 'the emergence of a space of flows which dominates the historically constructed space of places, as the logic of dominant organizations detaches itself from the social constraints of cultural identities and local societies through the powerful medium of information technology.' This space of flows integrates the informal city into the formality of the global process and context.

INFORMALITY IN THE FORMAL PLANNING PROCESS

The formal city-planning process in the tradition of positivist thinking has been understood as a top-down approach producing a spatial order as one more form of social control of the state. Urban planners mandated by the state or the local government are called to develop blueprints from their formal bureaucratic standpoints for later implementation. The outcome, whether streets or buildings or any other type of built environment, is supposed to reflect the vision of the urban planners.

This form of regulatory planning is based on power and produces the formal urban space for the expression of formal behaviors. There is then an adequation between formal structure and formal behavior. This emphasis on formality has obscured the role of informality in the planning process, although the expression of informality has been observed within the structure or context of the built-up environment.

However, informality has really always been part of the planning process in its triple manifestation: the design of blueprints, the implementation of policies and the lived experience of the urban residents. It is Uzzell's (1990: 114) view that there are two kinds of planning: generative and regulative. Regulative planning is based on power, is coercive and belongs to the domain of the formal sector. Generative planning, in contrast, is information-based with local knowledge and feedback and belongs to the domain of the informal sector.

Seeing formality and informality as part of a continuum rather than two separate entities or two different sectors, I propose that in the US city system there are two faces of the same coin of city planning. In this perspective, regulatory planning is also based partly on informality as the process and the outcome may depend on informal negotiations between policy-makers and local residents. The public façade may be formal but the process that leads to it may be fraught with informality.

Generative planning is not necessarily informal. Individual local residents or groups sometimes manage to impose their own agenda in specific areas of city development over the agenda of the city government. The activists of People's Park in Berkeley have fought to maintain the park over the city and University objections. They have used an informal networking to set a status quo agenda for the park. In San Francisco, residents have directed the city to redirect bus routes in their neighborhoods.

Urban planning has become part of a political process where both formality and informality interface to produce a negotiated, desirable outcome. Informality is at work in the top-down approach from conception to implementation even if it takes a back seat. Informality is more visible in the generative planning process or bottom-up approach, where formality may not be the driving force for its success.

The outcome of urban planning reflects the informality and formality of the process and provides a site or multiple sites where individuals can express their informal behaviors. The formal planning process cannot escape informality either in the design and implementation of blueprints or in its outcome. One may say that the formal outcome is a producer of informality.

Bureaucratic planning is regulatory planning: it is external and state-imposed with related application in the city. In contrast, informal planning is individual and community-based in that the thinking and the application evolved are controlled by the locals. In cities where residents live in areas that are under zoning regulations, the people have less room to engage in massive informal planning than in areas invaded by squatters. In the San Francisco metropolitan community, informal planning tends to concentrate in the home and the office (remodeling, for example) where individuals may bypass city regulations. It is informal planning because it is not regulated by the state approved bureaucratic system.

INFORMAL SPACE AS A SOCIO-POLITICAL PHENOMENON

Because it is so much linked to formal space, informal space is not only a social construction, but also a political phenomenon. Foucault (1980: 150) speaks in this regard of the 'politics of space' to suggest that 'anchorage in a space is an economico-political form'. Informal space has a political meaning precisely because it occupies a subjugated structural position *vis-à-vis* formal space.[3]

The informal space provides an infrastructure for the learning, use and transmission of informal knowledge. It provides a framework, a terrain for the expression of such knowledge. It is the locus where one learns the mechanisms for one's socialization in the world of informal practices, of behind-the-scene strategies and of differences in self-management style between formal and informal behaviors.

Informal space allows one to defy, adjust to or reinforce the formal system of power. Individuals who resist the entrenchment of the formal system take over informal space for the expression of a 'dissident subculture' (Scott, 1990: 108). This form of sub-jugated informal space allows for a bottom-up approach to locate oneself *vis-à-vis* state power.

Informal space can also work toward an adjustment of people to the power structure of society. It becomes then a safety valve for the strengthening of the formal system. To the extent that individuals can create informal space to solve their problems, they can return to the formal system, which remains unchallenged, to continue their journey.

MAKING SOCIAL SPACE FOR INFORMAL PRACTICE

People routinely make social space for informal practices. Informal space is often created inside formal space for this venture. The development of informal niches sustains the expression of informal practices. The multiplicity of these formal niches is made possible by actors who appropriate the space and transform it for that purpose.

Informal social space can be created in homes, public places and public buildings. Being informal at home is an acceptable practice by which one can reaffirm the self from any entrenchment by the formal system.

Taverns and cafés, while formal places, tend to be places that are informalized by those who frequent them. Here is a formal place that calls for or invites informal behavior. Formal space does not necessarily lead to formal behavior; it can also foster informal behavior that in turn transforms it into an informal space.

Public space can also be transformed into informal space without state interference. In San Francisco, Hispanic residents double-park on Dolores Street and around some churches as an informal way to reappropriate the formal street. Police do not interfere with this practice and do not give out tickets when this is done on Sunday mornings or Wednesday evenings. The formal apparatus tolerates the informal way, and city rules are thus bypassed by the informal sector. The informal here is a means to achieve a formal goal: attending church. When the formal is too rigid, the informal makes space for itself. The informal provides a solution to the formal. One sees here that a lack of articulation between city regulations and the requirements of other institutions in any society can be overcome by the mediating role of spatial informality.

INFORMAL SPACE AS SUBJUGATED SPACE

Just as we understand the informal sector as a pole of a continuum, we have proposed throughout this chapter that informal space requires the existence of formal space. In this sense, we may say that informal space is also 'polarized space' (Santos, 1979), implying its subjugated status *vis-à-vis* formal space.

The purpose of the creation of informal space by subordinate groups is to distance themselves from the dominant group, to communicate among themselves and to resist the infringement of the dominant sector on their lives. Informal space becomes than *oppositional space* in that it provides a niche to carry out oppositional politics and a base for resistance. Scott (1990: 118) notes that:

> The subordinate group must carve out for itself social spaces insulated from control and surveillance from above. If we are to understand the process by which resistance is developed and codified, the analysis of the creation of these offstage social spaces becomes a vital task. Only by specifying how such social spaces are made and defended is it possible to move from the individual resisting subject ... to the socialization of resistant practices and discourses.

An individual's movement from formal to informal space is not always willed: there may be a level of unconsciousness involved, or structural constraints from society. Separating those who remain in the formal space from those who occupy an informal space may not always be the best way of analyzing the process since the same individual can do both. What is new in this perspective is the recognition that those restricted to an informal space are able to communicate, orient and police themselves. I tend to agree with Scott (1990: 118) when he states that 'as domains of power relations in their own right, [informal spaces] serve to discipline as well as to formulate patterns of resistance.'

It is important to note the existence of 'a continuum of social sites ranged according to how heavily or lightly they are patrolled by dominant elites' (Scott, 1990: 120). It is true that there are sites where the informals are harassed and others not. While the former may be forced to formalize their ventures, the latter are more likely to continue to survive as informals. This is the case with street vendors.

Geographical distance may not be necessary to separate formal from informal space. Informal space may be located interstitially in formal space as long as the informals are able to communicate among themselves and to hide the content of their communication from the views of their counterparts. For Scott (1990: 120), 'the creation of a secure site for the hidden transcript might, however, not require any physical distance from the dominant so long as linguistic codes, dialects, and gestures ... [are] deployed.'

Informal space has its own characteristics and its multiple role can be debunked. It is a site where society can be criticized, an organizational site for resistance, a site for the recruitment and socialization of others, a site that provides an alternative to the formal site, a site for the 'transmission of popular culture ... and a site of antihegemonic discourse' (Scott, 1990: 121–2).

If the formal space is the realm of hegemonic practices, informal space is the realm of subjugated practices. In this sense, one may speak of a dialectic of tension between both ends. Subjugated space has the double characteristic of both subversion where one gathers to resist formal power and safety valve as it allows dissidents a niche to escape from the overcontrol of formal power.

Notes

1. For analyses on the reproduction of formal space, see Lefebvre (1974), Gottdiener (1988).
2. On the relations of 'telecommuting' and the 'electronic cottage' to the workplace, see Nilles (1976) and Toffler (1980).
3. To understand the way gender is a significant variable in the decoding and deconstruction of formal and informal space, see, for example, Spain (1992), McDowell (1983), Masson (1984), Wekerle et al. (1980), Zelinsky et al. (1982) and Mackenzie (1987).

3

The Informal Economy

The economic life of the informal city is sustained by the formal and informal aspects of the urban economy. It is so because the two sides of the urban economy are intertwined. To understand the behavior of the informal economy, it is less important to look at the outcome as Hart (1973) did when he spoke of it as an 'income generating opportunity', or as a sound basis for engineering development policies as De Soto (1990) does. It is important to focus on the process of its constitution and its relations to the formal aspect of the urban economy.

The informal urban economy covers a wide range of economic activities. Some are labeled by the state as illegal economic transactions, such as the 'numbers game' and drug trafficking. Others are informal, not because the activities *per se* are illegal but because those who are carrying them out, such as undocumented aliens, child labor and unlicensed professionals, are not able to do so legally, or because earnings are not reported to the state for tax purposes (Archambault and Greffe, 1984: 6). One must also add what Smith and Wied-Nebbeling (1986: 2) refer to as 'the non-market productive activities of households and voluntary organizations'.

Some are engaged in the informal economy as their permanent or exclusive source of earning hard currencies, others as a moonlighting practice. Still others are squarely located inside the formal system but open up interstices in it so as to carry out their informal practices, such as insider trading (Smith, 1990; Clark, 1988).

From a processual standpoint the intermingling of both sides of the urban economy becomes more obvious.[1] The informal and formal economic process seldom contains exclusively one or the other, but rather it is a flexible mix of both. Production may be initiated in the informal sector and the final product sold in the formal, or vice versa. Such is the situation in the informal sweatshop industry. It can be initiated in the formal, as a front business, carried out in the back-stage area (informal production) and returned back to the formal for the exchange to take place.

Somewhere in the production, distribution, marketing or transaction processes, it is likely that some forms of informality will creep in. The issue may be just to identify where it exists and how it relates to the formal side. An exclusive focus on either the formal or the informal cannot explain fully the process. The key to our understanding of the meshing of both still remains in the relationship between them since they belong to the same urban economy. It is the relationship that feeds, constrains and regulates. It provides a ground for the expansion or the constriction of one or the other.

In the past two decades, we have witnessed a proliferation of classifications or typologies in the study of the informal urban economy. These typologies are constructed to show the widespread nature of these practices (Henry, 1981), to show that they are not confined to the poor and immigrant communities (Portes et al., 1989) and to show that they are found both in the formal and informal economy (Ferman et al., 1987). The cataloguing of these practices, when they are accompanied with ethnographic descriptions, sheds much light on the process of their constitution. As far as typology goes, it could be helpful also to account for economic activities that are not impregnated by any informal process, if such exist.

Those who study the informal side of the urban economy from the perspective of the formal system tend to be interested in policy issues (Sethuraman, 1981). It is by no accident that the bulk of studies on the informal economy is done on underdeveloped countries. They are attempts to resolve the problem of urban poverty and unemployment by focusing on the survival strategies of the poor and their self-employment tactics (Turnham et al., 1990).

The location and identification of the informal sector has been an important goal of policy developers.[2] In the overwhelming majority of studies, it is this policy aspect that constitutes the angle through which the informal economy is defined and analyzed. The discussion has been connected with development because of the visibility of the phenomenon in third-world cities.

This perspective had led some to the erroneous conclusion that the informal sector is the result of rural–urban migration (Van Dijk, 1986).

The informal economy is often proposed as a viable development alternative to the formal sector, which is seen as being crucified by a moribund, complicated and elitist bureaucracy. In contrast, the informal is viewed as a dynamic, evergrowing sector that could become ever more progressive in a deregulated environment. De Soto's *El Otro Sendero* (The Other Path) summarizes well the positive view of this group of researchers and proposes the informal economy route as a way out of underdevelopment in Peru in particular, and in the third world in general.

Another trend of research carried out in the underground economy in the United States, Great Britain and Germany is a concentration not on its contribution to society, but on its negative side. Here the informal economy is seen as the villain that undermines the growth of the formal economy and prosperity of society (Tanzi, 1982). It is seen in this light at least for three reasons: (1) because it competes with the formal economy in terms of clientele and production of goods; (2) because the actors do not pay taxes on these transactions; and (3) because it is the domain where criminal elements excel (Harding and Jenkins, 1989; Shankland, 1980). For those who hold this view, the ultimate solution would be to eliminate this sector altogether by way of regulation.[3]

In between these two opposite trends, there is a large array of research perspectives. Most notable is the work of those who focus on the reciprocity and self-help aspects of these informal economies. Even before the term informal economy was coined, there were already numerous studies on mutual aid, barter and the social exchange aspects of neighborhood economies (Mauss, 1954; Davis, 1973). These studies are directly interested in understanding and explaining economic solidarity among individuals in the same neighborhood or among those who belong to the same ethnic group.

Some social scientists attempt to differentiate the various forms the informal economy takes, and to separate it from the formal economy. Rose (1983: 5) distinguishes the 'official' from the 'unofficial' and 'domestic' economies. He considers these to be 'three analytically distinctive economies'. Others argue that the informal economy is far from being monolithic and prefer to identify the distinguishing features of its various types. The informal economy is characterized as comprising the following: pre- or non-industrial economies. The household economy, the neighborhood or mutual-aid economy, the alternative or counter-culture economy, small enterprise and the black, underground or hidden economy (Ross and Usher, 1986: 31–3).

Still others show that the informal economy does not belong exclusively or is to be found only in the so-called 'informal sector', but is located as well in the formal sector. These researchers provide descriptions of economic activities in large formal or small semi-autonomous enterprises such as construction, public transportation, garment manufacturing, electronics, auto repair and furniture-making. Their work indicates that informal activities are part of the functioning of the operation of the formal system, whether in New York City, Madrid or Bogotá, Columbia (Benton, 1986, 1990; Sassen-Koob, 1989; Lanzetta de Pardo, 1989).

Within the boundaries of the American city, there are countless numbers of transactions that take place in the informal economy (Jones, 1988). Already, in the previous chapter, we have seen the impact of the informal economy on urban space. It is one factor that leads to the informalization of the urban space. In this chapter, the focus is on the deconstruction of the various ways in which the relations between the formal and the informal economy are articulated. The generative mechanisms by which the informal side of the urban economy regulates the formal aspect will be expounded.

Both boundaries and boundary maintenance can be enforced by both the formal and the informal sector. One is constantly infringing on the domain of the other. Examples from the informal economy are drawn to explain the process. It is obvious that the informal system is regulated by the formal system since formal laws are developed and implemented by the formal system. But what is not obvious is the fact that the informal system regulates the formal system as well.

When one speaks of the informal system as a regulatory system, what does one mean? It means that the informal has a generative capacity to regulate the formal system. It is informal regulation that one may distinguish from formal regulation. One presupposes that informal and formal actors are engaged in the same field of activity, and that each has the capacity of expanding its arena at the expense of the other. The informal appears to be an arena for the expression of repressed human freedom and a reaction against the overreaching arm of formalization.

The regulatory character of the informal system is the process by which it expands itself by creating new forms and encroaching on the formal system's arena. It regulates the formal system in the sense that it has the capacity to expand and shift its boundaries at the expense of the formal system. Constantly the informal economy is encroaching on the preserved domain of the formal economic sector, forcing the formal economy to concentrate on lawful activities and more expensive products and labor services. It thereby reduces the domain of practice of the formal economic sector. This is accomplished by a multitude of professionals who provide cheap products and services, and also by legitimate and formal businesses which partly follow the informal route to save money through hiring informal or extending operations into home shops or sweatshops.

Also regulatory is the process by which the informal system pressurizes the formal system to adjust itself to a *fait accompli*. This is done either by inclusion or exclusion. Adjustment is said to be inclusive when the formal system opens its border to co-opt or give formal status to the informal system.[4] It becomes exclusive when the informal system is seen as undesirable and rejected as illegal or is simply tolerated by the formal system. The informal system is thereby forcing the formal to question and adjust the edge of its boundary.

The regulatory phenomenon is expressed through the phenomena of boundary expansion, constriction or maintenance. The presence of the informal system pressurizes the formal system to redefine itself in terms of affirming its present, previous or new boundaries. Cases of informal economic activities in the San Francisco-Oakland Metropolitan Area are selected and analyzed to show the regulatory function of the informal sector.

AN INFORMAL GARDENER

The relationship between the informal and the formal sectors are here studied through the prism of a gardener, an informal professional who sells his labor and services to the formal sector. This is the story of a Mexican-American man who starts working in the formal sector for a salary and then decides to move to the informal sector so that he can be on his own, and also because he did not like his former cooking job in San Francisco.

His formal job consisted of cooking at a restaurant in the business district. This was a full-time job, with no possibility for advancement, and he held it for about ten years. While at the job, he maintained an informal operation of gardening for a few clients. Since he was at work for most of the week, he ended up doing his gardening jobs at weekends. Because of health problems, he reduced his time at the restaurant while augmenting his hours on informal jobs. From a full-time job at the restaurant, he moved to part-time. This gave him enough time to perfect his gardening skills, build up a clientele through his contacts at the restaurant, and purchase a truck. Finally, he decided to leave the restaurant job altogether and dedicate himself to gardening as an informal professional. He had learned of the possibility of developing his own informal business from a white gardener in the neighborhood, and from informals who had been hired on occasion to wash dishes in the restaurant who did gardening on their own. In this specific instance, the formal job was used as a stepping stone to land a job in the informal system.

We have here two patterns of informality. On the one hand, there is an individual who participates in both the formal and informal sectors to augment his salary. He is a cook in the formal sector, and a gardener in the informal. This means also that he has divided his time into that spent in the formal sector and that spent in the informal. On the other hand, we see that formal businesses like restaurants divide their activities into those performed by formals and those performed by informals. This latter strategy is used, of course, to lower costs. In the restaurant, the formal activity of dishwashing is handled by informals. A formal business may not operate totally with the use of formal labor. The informal appears here as an *enclave* in the formal sector.

The informal gardener was a generalist, not a specialist. After buying the secondhand truck, he later replaced it with a bigger truck that had an automatic device to make it easier to dump garbage. He also owned a lawnmover and an edger, plus other ordinary tools. He did mainly lawn jobs for regular clients and charged a monthly fee of about $50 for an average yard. For occasional clients, he charged according to the size and the length of time it might take to finish the job.

The money he made from working at the restaurant in the formal sector was invested in a truck to work in the informal sector. And the money he made in the informal sector he used to feed the formal sector, by paying his monthly rent.

As an informal gardener, his clientele came from the formal sector. He started by working his way through the neighborhood with older folks. There was not a lot of money involved, but it was practical because they lived nearby. He did this kind of job at weekends while he was still working for the restaurant.

When he became a full-time gardener, he was less and less interested in doing neighborhood jobs. He could get more money working outside the community. In addition to the contacts he made while at the restaurant, he started advertising through word of mouth. This constituted his *informal and main form of publicity*.

However, he is now able to get clients from a white gardener, who works for a firm in the formal sector. She is a licensed gardener, who works and functions mostly in the formal sector through her job at an institution of higher education. She also has a number of steady clients in the hills of San Leandro and San Francisco, but since she only does pruning, planting and watering she refers clients to him for lawnmowing or debris-hauling. One may say that through an *informal network*, he has been able to get jobs and enlarge his clientele in the informal sector.

He builds up his clientele by way of word of mouth. He goes about doing work for a family, and the neighbors may hire him to do the same. A job well done is in itself a form of publicity. Sometimes they do not see him on the job, but once the job is completed, neighbors may ask the family for his telephone number. This implies that he is a professional worker and his rates are fair and acceptable. Sometimes the neighbors inquire; at other times, it is the client who informs the neighbors about his availability. In this sense, the client from the formal sector can become an *informal advertising agent*.

Clients also come to him by way of referrals. Another gardener who specializes in specific jobs calls on him whenever he does not want to do a job, like hauling garbage to the dump site. Sometimes a gardener friend turns a job down and asks the client to call him, either because the desired rate is too low, or because he is too busy and this is not the kind of job he usually takes.

He uses other means to advertise informally. Sometimes he just leaves a leaflet in front of people's door in a given neighborhood. He has painted on his truck the words 'gardening and hauling', plus his telephone number. On still other occasions, he prepares posters which he staples to telephone poles hoping potential clients will locate him that way.

Over the years, the gardener has developed more clients through various means of publicity, all located squarely in the informal sector. Thus, to the formal publicity of the formal sector corresponds the informal publicity of the informal sector. Of course, the formal sector also uses informal publicity for its own ends.

Some clients are regular. The gardener works for them once or twice a month, or they call on him two to three times a year. Others are on a one-off basis; for example, when there is grass to cut or haul to the dump, he is given an opportunity to do the job.

To save gas, the gardener operates on the basis of his own subjective geographical divisions of the city. This is not formal geography, but rather an *informal geography* that he maps in his mind to correspond to his needs and work schedule. On the formal objective geography, he imposes his own. His geographical divisions or neighborhoods correspond to workplaces for him. All Berkeley jobs are done in one day, the San Leandro jobs in another day and the Oakland Hills jobs on yet another day.

The workplace is also a training ground for *informal apprentices*. Sometimes the gardener brings a son or a helper to the job. He gets training this way and in the process builds up a clientele of his own. After a few months, the apprentice may go on his own. He may, however, return to his *informal teacher* whenever he is unable to find work. This *informal training* leads to the informal sector of the economy. Through the informal training there is an *informal transmission of knowledge and skills* from one generation to the next. This informal training is fundamental to the social reproduction of informality.

In the domain of purchasing, one sees how the informal is intertwined with the formal. The gardener buys plants, tools, seeds and books from the formal sector for himself or the clients. Sometimes a client asks him to plant something. He either buys it from the store or takes it from his own *informal nursery* that he has developed at home. For example, he has sold to clients trees that he has planted in his own back yard. As an *informal producer*, he earns extra money by engaging in these informal economic transactions. All the money he makes, he spends on rent or to buy whatever he needs from the formal sector.

The informal gardener also subcontracts to take care of overflow of work. Once he fills his work schedule for the week, he may take on additional clients. He becomes then the manager of an *itinerant or informal firm* in the sense that he hires one or more people to do extra jobs. While he charges $40 per month for a small yard, he pays only $8 per hour to his employee and expects him to do the job in no more than two hours, assuming that he spends one hour every other week on the job. As an *informal manager*, he may supervise if he is doing another nearby yard. At the very least, he will check out the result before he pays his informal worker. In this way he maintains control over the output, makes extra money, enlarges both his clientele and profit and possibly his list of employees. Sometimes they are not employed to work independently, but only as helpers. This decision is made on the kind of work to be done, the availability of the *informal entrepreneur* and his level of trust in the employee. The transactions between the entrepreneur and the worker are paid in cash based on an *informal verbal contract*.

While the informal entrepreneur may give an inflated estimate in terms of the numbers of hours needed to complete the job, the employee cannot do the same to the entrepreneur since the latter has much experience behind him. The entrepreneur charges a flat fee while he pays his employee on an hourly basis. The informal entrepreneur is now making money in two distinct ways: in the work he does and the work he hires other people to do. This entrepreneurial practice is sometimes cyclical. Sometimes the informal does not have enough work to unload part of it on to someone else's shoulders.

The worker hired by the informal entrepreneur may be simply a person in training, a son or an acquaintance. We find illegal aliens hiring other aliens of the same ethnic group to work that way. However, it is also common to find a permanent resident or citizen exploiting alien labor this way. While the person is in training he may not get much in terms of cash from the entrepreneur, but he is getting a small wage and sometimes free shelter. These apprentices may develop their own clientele and move out on their own. Other informals may be hired just to help with certain kinds of work but do not wish to become engaged in gardening as a permanent way of making a living. Others are gardeners who specialize in a specific form of work and do not have enough clients to keep them busy. Whenever they have some free time, they may agree to work for another gardener for less money than they would make if it was their own client.

The *informal itinerant firm* functions like any formal firm. The entrepreneur is expected to have skills that will allow the operation to be successful. He is a manager, an accountant, a worker and a decision-maker. Sometimes a wife plays the role of secretary, getting messages, working out schedules and fixing prices. At times she does the work of manager and accountant as well. The home becomes then the headquarters of the firm, the site where administrative activities take place. This corroborates an earlier finding by Silver (1989: 118) who notes that 'many have jobs that take them to a variety of workplaces, leaving administrative activities to be performed in the home.' One must see informal gardeners as firms competing among themselves for clients and for their hegemonic practices in controlling neighborhood yards.

The interaction between the formal and the informal is carried out at various levels. Two examples will suffice here. The gardener hurts himself through an accident while working in someone's yard. The homeowner calls his insurance company, which pays $90 to a physician for his treatment as this kind of accident is covered by the homeowner's insurance policy. Here the informal, while doing an informal job, has had his accident expenses paid for by the formal sector because the homeowner was insured. Here is a case of the informal taking advantage of the formal sector, or the formal sector rescuing someone from the informal.

In the process of doing the informal job in the informal economic sector, the gardener/haulier also enters the formal market. He charges $20 for a dump, and part of this money is used to pay the dump site which is regulated by the formal sector. There is an intermingling here between the informal status of his practice and his transactions in the formal system. This is an informal practice that operates simultaneously in the formal and informal sectors.

INFORMAL MECHANICS

The entry of informal mechanic into the profession is achieved in two major ways. Mechanical repair is learned either in the informal sector or in the formal sector. When the skills are acquired informally, often the person learns by himself through playing with cars or from a family member, friend or acquaintance.

In one instance, we found an individual who had learned these skills from his father and then found work in the formal sector. In fact, the three African-American mechanics we interviewed all work in the formal sector. For them their work as a mechanic is not the basic source of their income. It is supplementary, except when they do not have a job in the formal sector.

Two of these three learned their skills in the informal sector and were able to get jobs in the formal sector as mechanics in a garage. Their father was a kind of jack of all trades and they went with him whenever he was asked to repair someone's car. The people in the neighborhood knew that they fixed cars and they did the job either in their own driveway, the client's driveway or wherever they could find a spot.

In one case, a client reports that she drove her car to the mechanic's house, brought the parts and he provided the labour. He did not charge anything because her boyfriend worked for the 'junk yard' and could get parts cheaper for him. The junk yard is for the informal mechanic what Grand Auto, an auto parts store, is for the formal mechanic, that is a place to acquire parts.

Working for a garage, another informal mechanic will also do work on the side. As a formal employee in the garage he depends on conditions imposed by the boss. When he is at home, however, he works for himself. He fixes neighbors' cars with minor troubles, although owners with cars that require access to special tools are referred to garages in the formal sector. Sometimes he rents special tools from the formal sector or borrows them from another informal. The junk yard also plays a significant role in the acquisition of parts. It is basically an *informal market* where a mechanic can come and buy cheaply parts that are still usable from junked cars. This is a recycling process whereby these parts are used to revitalize other cars. In this example, we are able to identify not only the *informal professional* and the *informal garage* (i.e. the place where he fixes cars) but also the *informal store* or the junk yard. The informal store functions on urban land run by an *informal shopkeeper*. Cars that cannot be fixed easily are dumped there. Parts from these cars are sold by the shopkeeper for a nominal fee.

Another informal mechanic, who learned his skills from his father, took over his father's clients when the old man died and developed his own clientele. Although he now works as an informal mechanic, he prefers to work in the formal sector as a matter of taste and reliability of income. Working part time for a warehouse in San Leandro three days a week, for the remaining part of the week he works in the informal sector.

As an informal mechanic, he works basically at the client's house. Sometimes he brings the car to his own house. His front yard, or the yard or driveway of his client, is used as an *informal garage* to fix the car. Sometimes he even drives the car to the junk yard where he can try different parts until he finds something that fits. There are two junk yards that he goes to – one in West Oakland and the other in Hayward – and buys parts there to save money.

He charges his clients on the basis of his estimate of labor time and the cost of whatever he may buy cheaply from the junk yard is passed on. However, the client may decide to purchase the parts himself, while paying the mechanic only for labor. To

replace an engine costs between $175 and $225, to tune it up costs
$20. This is evidently pocket money, and no tax is paid on this
transaction as it is not reported to the Internal Revenue Service.
The money is also sometimes used to pay rent and utilities. This
man estimates that when he is not employed in the formal sector
he makes approximately $200 per week.

Clientele come mainly by word of mouth. Sometimes people
for whom he has worked send clients to him coming basically
from the neighborhood and outlying areas. He recalls that former
clients who had moved to Richmond continue to provide him
with work and new clients. The outmigration of clients has led to
an extension of his work to other neighborhoods in Oakland and
nearby cities.

He is also part of a network of informal mechanics. He says he
interacts with four other mechanics, who refer people to him,
help him with advice or lend him tools. He also buys parts from
them. When they have too much work for a week, they ask him
to do some of it. Whatever money he makes, he keeps, although
he does not always receive cash for his labor. Sometimes it is
simply part of an exchange of services. He fixes the car of a
student neighbor and the student cuts the grass in his yard.

The mechanical skills he learned in the informal sector were
very useful in his search for employment in the formal sector. He
landed a job as a car-stereo installer in a place that specializes in
this kind of work, though he continues to fix the cars of his
neighbors. When he works full time in the formal sector, he
works as a mechanic at the weekend. He is known in the neighborhood and people constantly call on him.

The contract is made orally and he only takes cash. If there is a
disagreement, he tries to get the client's family members
involved. If the problem cannot be solved at this level, he may
leave with the understanding that he will not work for this
particular client again.

Sometimes he takes a client's car to a formal garage so he can
use the special tools there. The garage charges him $15, so even
the garage owner in the formal sector is getting some money
from the work the informal does in the informal sector. A portion
of the formal garage space is informalized at times as the
informal mechanic establishes an enclave to carry out his

informal mechanic's work. This shows the elasticity and the bi-functionality of formal urban space.

Here again we find the informal sector is tied to the formal sector at various levels. The client from the formal sector requests labor from the informal. Money is taken from circulation in the formal sector in exchange for services in the informal, and money that is made in the informal sector is invested in the banking system of the formal. Transactions made in the informal sector for labor are carried out in the garage squarely located in the formal sector while parts are acquired in the formal sector to complete work done in the informal. Skills learned in the informal sector are used in the formal, and skills learned in the formal sector are used in the informal to earn extra dollars. People who have worked full time in the formal sector fall back on informal jobs when they become unemployed.

INFORMAL CARPENTERS

Informal carpenters tend to work in most areas of construction. Within the construction industry, some are jacks of all trades. One Anglo-American informal carpenter who also worked as a carpet layer told me that he had learned his skills from his brother-in-law in England when he was 14 years old, though he had come over to America as a musician. When he reached the San Francisco Bay Area, he started by doing painting jobs, for example the interior of a building that housed a voluntary organization. One of the reasons that he was offered the job, and one of the conditions of the contract, was that he employed local African-American people. He complained: 'It was not very successful for me because I did not know any black people. There are a lot of black folks who come around here. They constantly pass by and let it be known that they are looking for work. For the ten blacks I hired, the work done was not very encouraging. That's a symptom of the area.'

How did he get his clients? He was first hired by a formal contractor who had met him at an *informal dinner party*. It was at that dinner that the *informal contract* was struck and concluded during the following week.

When he started, he had not at that point in time advertised himself as a painter in the neighborhood, though he felt he could handle the job successfully. The job lasted about three months and people in the neighborhood got to know him as a painter, asking as they passed by if they could borrow a brush from him, a ladder, or spare can of paint. They already recognized his dog and car because he had moved to the neighborhood four months earlier. He became a part of the community, recognized not only as a resident in the neighborhood but also as a worker just by his presence and was even asked if he could do different kinds of jobs. He noticed, however, that there was not a lot of money around and people were surprised at the amount he expected per hour. He had worked previously for upper-middle-class home-owners in Marin county and Berkeley but to expect those rates now would have been professional suicide. He notes that:

Once I was in the area working and visible, then people would come to me. There are certain questions when you are inter-ested in employing somebody you ask. Then you come from different angles. Can you do this work? Do you have time to do the work? How much do you charge if I were to employ you? Most of the people in the area ask how much do you charge. At first, I did not get work from the locals except raised eyebrows. Having lived and made friends around, I started dropping my prices not simply in order to get work, but also because I basically want to work within this community.

I never advertised in the newspaper, on electric posts, church bulletin boards. I get the clients because the people know me. Word of mouth travels. I subcontract and work with various people who have extra work (construction companies and both formal and informal professionals). They call me up. I don't have a licence. The formal professional has a licence and hires me as an unlicensed person. He supervises my work if I am with him or I do it alone. Contractors do not tell you how much they are getting for the job. They simply offer you a fixed per hour fee and they tell you how lucky you are.

The contract is struck by word of mouth. A good client will tell friends about the informal professional and this kind of *informal publicity* helps enlarge the clientele of the informal. The product itself is a form of advertisement. The neighbor or friend who sees good work may want to hire the informal professional who did it.

Landlords may let the superintendent of a building do routine maintenance work. If the superintendent cannot do it personally, he may hire an informal through his network. Rental property with a resident superintendent is one area where plumbing, masonry, carpentry and electric work is often done by informals.

Formality is also intertwined with informality in the purchase of materials. The form it may take depends on what the owner knows about the job and on the credentials of the informal. Some clients prefer to give money to the informal so he can buy the material, some may decide to accompany the informal to the store, or may later review the receipts. Leftover material from another job can also be used. In this case, the worker may make the client pay for the material he brings to the site. Sometimes the informal goes to a warehouse in Emeryville or Berkeley to scavenge for good pieces of wood, in this way lowering the cost of overhead that the warehouse owner would have to pay for waste removal. The informal may find that companies transporting glass are also good for scavenging. These companies throw out the wood in their dumpsters and are glad to see people taking it away.

Such leftover material is also a source of income for the informal as he can sell it to the client for whom he is working. However, the wood is seldom ready to be transported to the work site and nails often have to be removed. Moreover, the informal must invest time in transport.

The ambiguity of the social status of the informal is clear to both the formal client and the informal professional. The former has little professional respect for the latter, and for the latter, there is a great risk of not getting paid. When this happens, formal ways of redress cannot be used because the activity may be considered illegal by the formal sector. The informal finds himself in a similar dilemma when he hires another informal for help. If this informal does not do a good job or steals tools, there is no way this problem can be solved through the courts. In this situation the channels of the *informal judicial system* have to be used.

Sometimes an informal is used to rescue a formal operation, for example a job for which a contractor has been paid but has left unfinished and not well done. An informal may be hired to complete the job, costing the owner less than if it were to be completed by the formal contractor. The informal may have more skills and be more reliable than the carpenter from the formal sector but has to work in this way because he happens to be an undocumented immigrant.

The *informal network* is the key to understanding the recruitment process, the finding of occasional jobs and the sharing of knowledge among peers. Recruitment is often promoted by way of friendship and apprenticeship. Informals provide jobs to other informals when they have too much work to complete in a given week, passing jobs to someone else in their network. At other times, a *generalist informal* may call on a *specialist informal*, like an electrician. The informal also gives jobs to formals. He may call on a specialist in the formal sector to do a job, to oversee the execution of a job or to inspect the job once it is done. There are also professionals who are aware of the existence of the *informal network* and who may call on informals for small jobs, hire them for specific jobs in order to lower overhead costs, or simply direct them to clients.

The work of the informal carpenter is not carried out exclusively in any specific neighborhood. Rather this type of informal is hired both inside and outside the neighborhood. Moreover, there are *lower-class* informals one must distinguish from *middle-class* informals. Many do not own a truck, a car or even the tools they need, but are hired by middle-class informals as helpers. Hence a *stratification system* is built into the informal sector itself.

STREET VENDORS

Throughout the San Francisco-Oakland Metropolitan Area we find many street vendors selling one form of product or another. Sometimes they stand in a specific place like a street corner. Others are itinerant, changing locations depending on the time of day or the day of the week, or simply canvassing from door to door. In the previous sections, we emphasized informal professionals who sell their services and informal activities closely linked to the formal sector. It is also important to analyze the interplay between formality and informality among street and open-air vendors.

Unlicensed street vendors are less visible in the American city than they are in the third world because they are more likely to be penalized by the state (Tinker, 1987). In the San Francisco Bay Area, street vendors sell a variety of items from handmade gift materials to cooked food. Their informal and itinerant businesses attract clients from every spectrum of the local population, as well as further afield.

These gift materials are made in home shops and sweatshops for the street operation. Not all home shops are backward- or forward-linked to a formal firm. Some follow the informal route and sell in *informal street markets*.

It is interesting to note that no ethnic group has any monopoly over this form of trade. Anglos, Asians, African-Americans, Native Americans and Latinos equally participate in it both as buyers and vendors. Latino street vendors can be seen selling T-shirts and sweatshirts to tourists at Union Square and Fisherman's Wharf in San Francisco. In a study of the Mexican-American community in East Los Angeles, it has been found that street vending is a widespread informal economic activity. Among the most common types are *los moscos* (flies), day laborers who stand in a specific area waiting to sell their labor to an informal employer, and the *mariachis* (Mexican musicians) who show up with their musical instruments and wait on a specific street corner to be hired for a party or by a bar, as well as the 'carriers', the 'asphalt vendors', the 'push-cart vendors', the 'tent vendors', the 'weekend vendors', the 'auto vendors' and the 'Roach Coaches' (large food trucks) (Rojas, 1991: 52–4). This elaborate classification was developed to show the distribution and specialization of Mexican-American street vendors in East Los Angeles. Rojas (1991: 52–4) further argues that these specializations, which may not be noticed by the larger public, constitute a circuit of informal communication between the vendors and prospective Latino buyers. To the informal communication in the mainstream culture corresponds an informal communication system within this ethnic minority culture.

Food vending also shows how the informal regulates the formal. Many people buy their lunches from vendors. This puts pressures on local restaurants to lower prices. In some instances, the vendor occupies a specific niche selling an exotic or ethnic minority food. At other times, he competes directly with the formal restaurant by selling the same items cheaper.

In the mainstream community door-to-door canvassing is carried out by school-age youngsters selling candies, for example. In the Oakland Cambodian community, it is carried out by women who sell mostly jewelry. Itinerant retailers develop a network of clients, and in the evenings and on weekends they visit the homes of compatriots to sell their produce to prospective buyers. Sometimes these products are handmade, sometimes not.

Flea markets and garage sales are other types of informal economic activities city residents engage in. Both serve as a place for the recycling of still usable but unneeded items. In the flea market, we find both licensed and unlicensed vendors, home and factory-made items, and new and secondhand merchandise. However, according to Lozano (1983: 351), 'because they are more likely to start out selling their own possessions and other used goods, they more often become specialized as junk dealers'. She has further found that 'personal belongings may be put up for sale and an item that is displayed for sale may be used at home during the week' (Lozano, 1983: 352). Flea markets and street vending are secondary markets that attract people in search of bargains. They serve as an extension to formal stores or formal sector firms. The latter feed them with their unsold merchandise and they provide in return an outlet for these hard-to-sell products.

While the flea market is a weekend event, the garage sale is more likely to be a seasonal or annual affair. Both allow the vendor an opportunity to make extra dollars. These activities take items purchased in the formal sector and resell them in the informal sector. This money is again used for transactions in the formal sector.

VISIBLE FIRMS AND INVISIBLE LABORERS

In the previous sections, the emphasis has been placed on informality in the informal sector. We now turn our attention to informality within the formal sector. It is our view that the formal sector functions also on the basis of informality, either by allowing the informal economy to flourish in its interstices or by extending its formal practices within or without the geographical boundaries of the firm.

In San Francisco, we find several Asian-American shops that specialize in the repair of televisions and other electronic products. These function as front businesses so that both formal and legal procedures are carried out in the open and in the shop. However, the work is actually done by informals in their residences inside or outside the city, and once the work is completed, the product is returned to the front business. This is why we call these laborers 'invisible' because they carry out their subcontracted work in the shadow of the formal sector of the economy. The front business could probably not survive without them.

We also find front-door businesses that serve to cover up backdoor businesses. A dining place will sometimes serve both as a formally approved restaurant and as a venue for the numbers game where players come to purchase their numbers and receive their winnings. The existence of the lottery attracts clients to the restaurant, and the money made in the racket business is used to help pay for the restaurant operation.

We also find firms in which some production is carried on in sweatshops. These are home industries making garments or fixing clothing. Such sweatshop firms are hired by formal firms specifically to provide these kinds of services which are provided by people from diverse ethnic and class backgrounds. Silver (1989), who has analyzed the US census, finds a link between subcontracting chains and the growth in illegal home work. She further notes that:

> Thousands of Hispanic and Asian homeworkers stuff circuit boards in Silicon Valley and are paid off the books. Subcontractors in San Francisco's Chinatown have set up hun-

dreds of garment industry sweatshops from which, it has been estimated, almost half the employees take work home to evade union rules. (Silver, 1989: 111)

In her research on the informal economy in the San Francisco Bay Area, Lozano (1989: 5) has found that 'these individuals are not driven by poverty and unemployment, but rather by tensions on the shop and office floor.' This is a kind of rebuttal of the generalization that one finds in most of the literature on the informal economy among the poor in the third world. For example:

Bank managers whose technical documentation requires constant maintenance arrange for manuals to be updated by former employees, now 'freelancing' as technical writers in their living rooms. The job that proves too demanding to complete without hiring extra employees is cheerfully accepted by the owner of the secretarial agency, and then sent out to one of her friends who has a wordprocessor at home. Even companies that provide sophisticated services such as computer programming and software development keep at hand in the Rolodex a listing of 'consultants', clever hackers who can be depended upon to get the program written, even if it means staying up for days at their home terminal (Lozano 1989: 5).

Sometimes, these operations are one-off affairs, sometimes they are more permanent. Computer work or television repairs carried out in a sweatshop fashion make up a flourishing industry in the San Francisco Bay Area. The high-tech industry has helped informal economic practices mushroom in the formal economy.

VISIBLE LABORERS AND INVISIBLE FIRMS

The formal firm is also a place where informal work is carried out that is *not* for the benefit of the firm. The formal operation is exploited by workers for their own benefit to augment their incomes. This kind of work uses two different assets from the formal firm.

The first form this practice takes is doing work in the informal sector at the place of employment. The paid time that is supposed to be for carrying out the firm's work is used to do work on the side. We find individuals who are employed in a formal firm bringing to the office their own editing and translation work. These informal jobs are carried out on paid time.

A second way workers use the firm's assets is by using its tools. This is clearly the situation of a secretary who uses company paper, typewriter, desk and space to type a client's dissertation. In this example, she functions in both the formal and informal sector at the work site. The office provides her a chance to engage in the informal economy. While the laborers are visible, the informal firms for which this work is carried out on the side are not.

Cuff, who has carried out field research in San Francisco and elsewhere in the nation, has found informal economic practices to be rampant in architectural firms. One area that has particularly caught her interest is that of moonlighting. Here we find that architects who are hired to do work for the formal sector are also engaged in informal economic practices, using their affiliation with the formal firm to establish legitimacy and the formal work site to complete work contracted in the informal arena. She notes that:

> Young, recently graduated architect-employees search for and accept moonlighting jobs – independent design projects completed outside the office – not only to make extra money but also to be able to make their own decisions. Moonlighting keeps 'business' at the office and provides an outlet for design. Sometimes it is a form of economic sabotage, as when architect-employees accept jobs from the same market that their office goes after. They are then in essence competing for work with their own employers. Firms can also be held liable for problems that occur in their employees' outside projects. For these reasons moonlighting is done clandestinely. (Cuff, 1991: 51).

FORMAL BUSINESS AND INFORMAL MERCHANDISE

In the products that are sold, we find yet another form of the mixture of formality and informality in the formal firm. Some products come from the formal sector and others from the informal. Both of them can be sold side by side in the formal shop.

The client who buys products from a store is not likely to be able to distinguish their origins so we find that informals who are unable to have their own shops for various reasons place their informal merchandise in formal shops. We have encountered this practice in San Francisco's Chinatown. The informal producer lets the shopowner sell the items, and shares with him or her the profit, an arrangement often made between family members and friends. The formal shop thus provides a niche so that products from the informal sector can be sold in the open formal-sector market.

THE REGULATORY CAPACITY OF THE INFORMAL SECTOR

The very existence of the informal sector points to a series of regulatory consequences *vis-á-vis* the formal sector. Because it is easy to enter the informal sector, it can expand, recruiting people from both the formal and informal sectors. For example, producers may come from the informal sector while buyers come from the formal sector or vice versa. An overflow of activities in the informal sector can lead to an expansion of the formal sector since 'informalists' who have accumulated enough money and skills can opt to function in both the formal and informal sectors. They can also switch altogether to the formal sector.[5] One reason why people do not enter the formal economic sector as entrepreneurs is because they do not have enough capital. In this mixed arrangement, the informal sector expands the domain of the formal sector by providing sufficient capital to allow informals to enter and enlarge the formal sector population, helping to maintain formal sector activities by decreasing overhead costs.

The informal sector may also help increase household consumption in the formal sector. All the new products created find a market or buyers in the formal sector. Increased household income is used not only to buy products from the formal sector, but also from the informal sector. However, the informal sector sometimes reduces the availability of certain products to the formal sector. It thus has the capacity of either reducing or enlarging the content of household consumption in the formal sector.

Since the goods produced in the informal sector are not for the exclusive use of the informal sector but are also for the formal sector, this brings a new regulatory element into the picture, that of competition. This competition affects the formal system in different ways and at different levels.

One manifestation of competition arises in terms of the goods being circulated in the market which may be different from those available in the formal sector or the same types of goods but cheaper. In either case, it dissuades buyers from the formal sector and consequently decreases the level of profit that could be earned by the formal sector.

To the extent that the informal sector can make the same kinds of goods available to buyers, the formal sector is put under pressure to adjust its prices. If the formal sector decides to ignore the informal sector, the latter will continue to attract buyers who otherwise would have stayed within the formal sector.

Moreover, with the existence of an informal sector, the formal sector must compete for clients, and could lose them to the informal sector.

On the other hand, the formal sector may produce inferior goods for low-budget clients that compete with those in the informal sector. In this case, competition occurs in a targeted portion of an already segmented market.

The informal sector can sometimes even force a specific firm to move out of a neighborhood, if new ethnic residents move in and prefer to buy from their own informal markets.

One area where the informal sector is in sharp competition with the formal sector is in unskilled labor. Some unskilled laborers in the informal sector are there precisely because immigration laws prevent them from participating legally in the formal economy. They are hired to do odd jobs like gardening in private homes or dishwashing or maintenance work in formal business settings.

As Lozano (1983: 359) notes, 'this competition results in increased pressure on the state to enforce business ordinances and to draft additional regulatory legislation.' The formal sector forces the state to regulate the boundaries of these enclave activities, because they expand and overflow into formal sector activities.

The informal sector may be the first to provide a solution to a need felt in the community. Street food vending is a case in point. The formal sector then comes along and either rejects or accepts the solution and integrates it into the formal sector. The informal sector thus forces the formal sector to set guidelines and policies concerning street vending, and to expand its control of the urban economy.

The informal sector also contributes to the maintenance of ethnic enclaves because it produces the ethnic goods consumed in that enclave. If it were not for these ethnic goods, those in the ethnic enclave would become full-time consumers in the formal sector.

THE INFORMAL ECONOMY OF THE INFORMAL CITY

Throughout our analysis, the aim has been to conceive, understand and explain the economic basis of the informal city. Informality is found not only in the so-called informal sector, but in the formal sector as well. This led us on to distinguish and show the existence of informality in the urban economic process, and its generative impact on the formal side of the economy.

From a structural standpoint, informality is seen in the interstices of the formal economy, either as an enclave or as an extension of the formal economy. Evidently, the way in which the informal is linked to the formal is finely nuanced. The interstitial niche occupied by the informal within the boundaries of the formal economy helps smooth the functioning of the formal economy. That informal function is produced by the formal for formal ends.

The informal economy is seen as an extension of the formal economy when parts of the production are carried out in sweatshops, for example. As an extension, it can be related to the formal economy through a backward or forward linkage process. This linkage can be direct, that is without mediation, or indirect through a third agency.

The informal economy exists also as an enclave. In the formal firm, there may be individuals who use the facilities to carry out informal economic activities. Using the office wordprocessor to type texts for an outside client is a case in point. We find similar examples in hospitals and among cooks in the hotel industry.

The informal economy is also seen as peripheral in the sense that it allows the poor to get by in difficult times and other city residents to get cheaper services. These activities allow the individuals to survive and to function in the formal economy.

However, it is proper to correct one current fallacy. The general view that goods and services produced in the informal economy are cheaper than similar ones in the formal economy is not always true. To understand this, one must look at five different variables: (1) the cost factor – that is, the cost of the item compared to that of a similar item sold in the formal sector; (2) the accessibility factor – can the same item be found nearby in the formal sector? If not, to the cost one must add distance and time expenses; (3) the immediacy factor – that is, the item may be needed now and it may not be possible to wait for tomorrow when the stores are open; (4) the belief factor – the purchaser may believe that the item is less expensive even if that is *not* the case; and (5) the quality factor – whether the item is handmade or factory made. On the basis of the variables mentioned above, we may conclude that the price may not necessarily be comparable.

The structural analysts want to maintain the distinction between formal and informal.[6] The interpretive or hermeneutic analysts, on the other hand, see the agent as moving from one side to the other. For the latter, it is difficult to figure out where the formal aspect ends and the informal begins because there is a human agent at the center linking both. When we bring in the notion of intentionality, this complicates matters further. The agent may use the informal mode for expediency in order to take advantage of an opportunity to strengthen his *formal* business. The human subject cannot be ignored in the process. He or she is the source or agent in the making of the urban economy.

Some see the formal and informal aspects as a single economy and reject the notion of two economies.[7] They continue to use the distinction because they think it to be, although unsatisfactory, nevertheless necessary. Couched in structural terms, this problem cannot be solved for three reasons: (1) these analysts focus on the outcome (money is made through this activity); (2) they identify informal activities as if they were separate from the formal; and (3) they compare them with more conventional ones and find them to be underground, illegal and small in size. When the problem is presented like this, no solution can be forthcoming. This has led so far to a great deal of confusion.

To understand the unified nature of the urban economy, one must see that the sectoral economic activities are part of a whole, and are tied to other sectors and the mainstream economy. This linkage with the formal economy becomes more obvious when we look at it from the angle of the individual actor. His informal economic activities are tied to the formal sector as goods and clients may be from that sector, and money made through these activities is used to pay rent or to buy services and goods in the formal sector, or simply to invest in the formal banking system.

In consequence, the informal side of the urban economy is not a separate sector. It is an interdependent and subjugated sector, from which, through a bottom-up approach, we may understand the inner working of the urban economy. The same individual may contribute to, or use, both aspects of the economy, and sometimes use one to enhance his chances in the other.

Everyday life usually displays both a formal and informal component. When we dislodge the informal practices and look at them as a system, we see clearly that they are part of the formal system. We simply look at the total system from the angle of the informal in the same way we could study a family from the angle of the children or the domestic servants, rather than that of the husband or the wife.

The formal and informal sides of the urban economy join each other in different ways. Sometimes their relations are dominant, interstitial, central or peripheral depending on the angle of study. The failure to see these different kinds of intermingling has led some to posit the informal sector as a separate phenomenon in a dual social system. This cannot be proven by empirical data. Analytically, it stands as an interdependent sector or an inter-stitial process in a pluralist economic structure. It owes its exist-ence and survival to its linkage to the formal sector. Thus the informal economy provides a basis or field of action for the actors of the informal city.

Notes

1. The network of contacts established for the nurturing of a market
    relationship or business may survive even after the loss of one's
    business. The informal economy then is in the business of pro-
    ducing informal relations which maintain their own autonomy.
    These informal relations, because they produce and share know-
    ledge, may be the locus that facilitates a re-entry into the formal
    economy.
2. The informal economy is seen in the policy realm as either a prob-
    lem or an opportunity. As an opportunity, it can be expanded and
    co-opted. It can also be recognized legally as a parallel structure.
    As a problem to be eliminated, the solution proposed rests with
    correcting the failure in the formal system that produces the
    informal sector and in the resocialization or the raising of the level
    of consciousness of the informals so that they can acquire the ways
    of the formal system.
3. Sauvy (1984: 276) discusses the three alternatives the state has in
    confronting the informal sector of the economy: '(1) réprimer, en
    renforçant les contrôles et en augmentant les peines, (2) tolérer, en
    estimant que l'optimum n'est pas dépassé, du moins pour
    certaines activités, (3) céder, en réduisant la charge fiscale'.
4. For Archambault and Greffe (1984: 25) three types of explanation
    concerning the cause of the growth of the unofficial economy have
    been provided. They refer to 'ajustement individuel', 'blocage du
    fonctionnement des marchés' and 'rapports de production'.
5. Van Dijk (1986: 26) sees the informal sector as 'transitional' in the
    sense that it serves as a stepping stone to capture a job in the
    formal sector.
6. Mittar (1988: 20–1) prefers to identify the informal sector 'in terms
    of the household to which the individual belongs'. He went on
    to identify the types of household he has found in his study:
    '(a) those belonging to the formal sector, (b) those belonging to the
    informal sector, and (c) those belonging to the mixed category'.
7. Harding and Jenkins (1989: 51) reject 'the notion of different econ-
    omies [while] retaining a distinction between formality and
    informality with reference to particular economic activities in
    specific social situations'.

4

Informality and Urban Politics

The daily political routine of the city provides us with several niches where we can productively understand and explain the informal side of urban politics. The informal city, in fact, is also sustained by the informal political system and administrative process. Urban politics has a visible and formal arena regulated by the formal political system. It has also an informal side which survives in the interstices of, or serves as an extension to, the formal system. This is why we need to explain the mechanisms of its production and relations with the formal system.

Political informality refers analytically to two distinct realities. On the one hand, one can think of an informal group that assembles on the basis of common goals with a view to bettering their plans and possibly influencing the course of the formal political system or city government. On the other hand, it refers to a procedure, a way of doing things, which may not follow a formal blueprint or set of formal rules.

In mapping the geography of informal urban political practices, we identify three niches that are important for our analysis: the informal political process as anchored through the actions of informal leaders at the grassroots community level, the informal process as played out within the confines of the formal system at City Hall, and the upward and the downward relations between the grassroots and the mayor's office or between the mayor's office and state and federal leaders.

What strikes any perceptive observer of the urban American social landscape is the vast density of politicking that goes on behind the scene. This is not done randomly, but rather consistently both in the formal political system and in the parapolitical system – even in the latter one finds even more behind-the-scene political maneuvers and activities. When it is well explained, this informal process can open the gate to a better understanding of the total system.

The informal political system is not a distinct entity totally separated from the formal system. This dual view of the political reality is not valid. The informal system is seen here 'not just as instrumental in the cause of an extensive formal power but as constituted by and within such power' (Fitzpatrick, 1988: 180). The difference in this formulation of the issue is that we see the urban political system as including a diversity of political spaces 'operating simultaneously on different scales and from different interpretive standpoints' (Santos, 1987: 288).

Durkheim (1960) was among the first social scientists who saw the need to explain the role of voluntary associations in society, especially in their relations to the formal state. He sees them fulfilling three major roles: (1) restraining the overarching arm of the formal state, (2) counterbalancing the power of the state, and (3) constituting an essential condition for the liberation, freedom and emancipation of the individual. Voluntary associations are not mechanisms created by the state but by groups of individuals to protect their interests, channel their views and values, and to influence state policies. Durkheim goes so far as to imply the existence of these secondary groups as a *sine qua non* in the practice of democracy.

Following the lead of Durkheim, Greer and Orleans (1962) see formal voluntary organizations as 'mediating organizations' (see also Merton, 1961: 112). They interpret their effectiveness in terms of their ability 'to mobilize the population in such a way as to limit the administrative state' (Greer and Orleans, 1962: 635). They refer to them as 'parapolitical' because such institutions are not derived from state institutions, but rather are produced by the local neighborhoods. These mediating formal voluntary associations are seen precisely as being parapolitical in the sense that they allow 'the translation of norms, commitments, and interests, into political behavior. For the individual citizen, political information, influence, and identification require such a sub-set of organizations in which he may participate' (Greer and Orleans, 1962: 635). What they say about formal voluntary organizations can also be said about informal voluntary organizations. This leads us to refer to informal voluntary organizations as informal parapolitical organizations.

However, our definition of the parapolitical structure is more inclusive than those proposed by Durkheim and Greer and Orleans; it must also include the informal network and means used by the city government, informal political discourse and ideology, and the informal administrative structure. The informal parapolitical structure is not simply a mediating mechanism, but is also the backbone that is ever-present in the everyday operation of the formal political system. It is central to the production of the urban political process.

Here the informal parapolitical system is seen as a processual system, a system in which motion and change constitute an essential element for its survival. Two types of change are envisioned here. One is internal in the sense, for example, that the repositioning of one element changes the relations of that unit to others. The other is external and depends on relations with the formal political system. Boundaries of the informal parapolitical system may shift because of changes in the boundaries of the formal system. Through this processual analytical standpoint, I will show that both the formal and informal aspects constitute the totality of the urban political reality. The separation of the whole into the informal and formal components is a heuristic device to better analyze the making and shaping of the processual outcome.

INFORMAL PARAPOLITICAL ORGANIZATIONS

The reality of parapolitical organizations has led researchers to seek the nature of their origins. Some have become more visible because the neighborhoods in which they emerged have been annexed, changing from an independent town into one of the urban neighborhoods of a megalopolis. In such a situation, 'once the official institutions of local government have been moved downtown, what remains of neighborhood governance is chiefly the informal, dispersed, and intermittent activity of political non-professionals' (Crenson, 1983: 11). What annexation does is to remove the formal political system to a different site, not the parapolitical players, even though the parapolitical structure must adapt to the new political reality.

The parapolitical organizations whose internal structure we are about to analyze have a different political origin. They are produced by or as a reaction to the formal system, coming into being because people want to preserve or improve the quality of life in their neighborhoods. In this sense, they can be seen as institutions that foster community values, that socialize people in the culture of democracy and that serve as mediating institutions *vis-à-vis* the formal system, and they provide both a forum through which formal leaders can challenge or be challenged by neighborhood residents and a platform for informal leaders who seek elective offices.

The neighborhood provides an excellent niche for the rise of informal leaders and the development of informal organizations. It is there that one can follow with some precision the appearance and disappearance, as well as the various forms and shapes of, informal organizations.

Grassroot organizations begin as informal organizations. Even after they have formalized their rules and procedures, the people may continue to use informal means to achieve their stated goals.

The existence of informal organizations within the city is a corollary to and vital to urban democracy. Throughout the history of the American city, there has always been a felt need – whether in a homogeneous white population or one with multiple ethnic groups – for residents to band together informally to influence the course of city policies and politics and to prevent the deterioration of their neighborhoods (de Tocqueville, 1945: 114–32; Tomeh, 1964).

The residents of West Oakland have a long history of participating in informal and grassroot organizations. Starting in the late 1930s, the city began to adopt a progressive policy of city improvement, the outcome of which was the changing face of the old West Oakland neighborhood. This was when residents banded together in what they called the West Oakland Planning Council to try to influence city policies (Hayes, 1972: 110).

This trend toward participation in neighborhood informal political organizations became much stronger after World War II as more African-Americans came to settle in Oakland. The white city council was little inclined or willing to listen to their concerns and needs. However, the informal political structure became more heterogeneous and well established as a product of the changing policies of the city, which evolved from its 'Redevelopment', 'Model Cities', and 'Economic Development' planning strategies. Informal leaders still living participated in all these various phases of the evolution and transformation of the informal parapolitical structure in this part of the city. They have worked very strongly in the informal structure to influence, lobby and help redirect the decisions that affect West Oakland.

The pattern of migration and resettlement has influenced the composition and dynamic of the informal groups in West Oakland (Daniels, 1980). The migrants from Texas, Louisiana, Alabama and Mississippi continue to maintain their informal group ties within the informal neighborhood group because of friendship or family connections. This common background has been a force to bring people together and also to build consensus through the leaders of each sub-group. Within the informal parapolitical structure, there is a grouping by states. This characteristic is, however, slowly declining with the younger generation.

Place of origin then is a marker in the composition of the informal group, helping in networking. People who share the same experience band together. Such groups are easy to galvanize because the people share a homogeneity of meanings and views.

The National Association for the Advancement of Colored People (NAACP), although a formal organization, also has its members that served or joined the informal organization. They may have joint activities, or some members may participate either on their own or as representatives of the organization.

The informal networks sometimes give rise to long-term acquaintances. Even when people move to the formal, those informal ties can be reactivated at any time. Not all the members may continue to live in the same neighborhood. Those who move out still have influence there. The 'informal machine' survives even after the emigration of members to other neighborhoods. With gentrification comes a recomposition of the informal demographic content of the informal sector.

In the metropolis, more than one informal political organization exists. In fact, there are several. Sometimes they are in
competition and at other times work in collaboration with each
other. Some individuals belong to more than one informal political organization. Informal parapolitical organizations are by
definition interest groups.

There is a certain element of elasticity among the membership
of informal groups. At a certain time of the year, when there is an
event, membership may be large. At other times, around an issue,
it may be small. Each leader brings his or her own constituency
when the informal group organizes a meeting around a common
cause. If a leader leaves the informal organization, he may take
the constituency out of the coalition as well.

The informal structure is not absolutely informal but includes
entities with formal structures as well. Such structures as the
West Oakland Development Council, Model City organizations
and the West Oakland Mental Health Board have formal structures but came into being because of pressures from informal
parapolitical groups. These formal structures are linked to each
other through informal networks of relationships.

Informal organizations with a generalist purpose tend to give
birth to informal organizations with specialist purposes, for
which they serve as an informal coordinating mechanism.
Among the latter, we find the Senior Citizens Council, Progressive Senior Citizens, the St Patrick's Council, the Acorn Revitaliza-
tion Council, the McClymonds Alumni Association, the
McClymonds Community Board, the Oak Center Neighborhood
Association and the Citizen Emergency Relief Team which was
formed to deal with the fallout from the Loma Prieta Earthquake.
All of these associations have as their goal the improvement of
life in West Oakland. To achieve that goal, they hold regular
meetings or maintain ongoing interactions with formal structures
such as the Oakland Redevelopment Agency, the Oakland City
Council, the Oakland Planning Association, the Oakland School
Board and the Peralta Community College Board.

These community organizations may have some formal structures, but they are run on an *ad hoc* informal basis. They are
linked to each other – and sometimes to the formal sector –
through informal means, and through their interactions with the

formal sector they have learned a number of lessons. The informants have reiterated three principles for a successful out-come to their interactions with the formal sector. The first is that they must be as well versed with the subject matter as the formal structure, and in many cases better versed. The second is that they must be consistently assertive and aggressive. (However, it is no longer necessary to be disruptive to attract the formal sector's attention as was the case during the decade of the civil rights movement.) The third principle is that informal organizations must have an agenda and a clear idea of what they want to accomplish.

Informal organizations are by definition soft organizations in that they are run informally but are forced to formalize their structures temporarily and cyclically so as to discuss their agendas. *The cyclical meetings allow them to formalize temporarily their structures so that they can express and reinforce the informality of their character.* This is why the informal organizations have regular meetings with regular agendas and regular items to take into account.

THE ETHNIC FACTOR

It is important to note that there are cultural differences in the way ethnic groups and communities employ informality in their relations with the formal political system. Cultural practices within ethnic communities tend to carry over into the relationship between grassroots and parapolitical organizations and the formal system of municipal government. Focusing on this aspect of *political informality* helps clarify how informal ethnic leadership differs.

In the African-American community the church is the central institution that sustains informal political organizations (Hamilton, 1972). Historically, the church has been controlled by African-Americans. It provides a setting to discuss ideas, a ground to organize protest, training for leadership and a point of contact between the community and the outside world, and it can trade the votes of the congregation for services to the community. The church is part of and central to the African-American parapolitical system.

Asian-American parapolitical organizations have a different dynamic because of the history of immigration to the Bay Area. Asian-Americans belong to national groups with distinct cultural practices, including distinct languages, and they maintain an interest in local politics and the political situation in their home countries.

Among the politically active Bay Area Asian-American groups are the Chinese, Filipinos, Laotians, Cambodians, Vietnamese, Japanese and Koreans. The Chinese are by far the most numerous and are the most vocal and articulate among the Asian-American groups in Oakland. They have their own Chinatown, even though it has become more and more an 'Asiatown', including many other groups.

Cambodians, for example, started to arrive in Long Beach, California, in the early 1970s, before the Khmer Rouge began their killing spree. These immigrants were mostly former officials. After Vietnam invaded Cambodia in 1979 many more peasants came. The Oakland segment is poorer and less sophisticated than the Long Beach Cambodian population.

In 1983, Cambodians established in Oakland the *Cambodian New Generation Inc.* (CNG). CNG is less active in local Oakland politics and more active in Cambodian politics. This reflects the reality that the majority of them are not American citizens. From peasant backgrounds, they worry that if they become citizens, they might lose the public aid they receive as refugees. Younger Cambodians connected with CNG are more active politically.

The informal Cambodian political system is part of a network of informal Asian-American political leaders. The Director of CNG was at the center of the process for three reasons: his office was highly visible and people depended on him for leadership; he represented the Cambodians at the East Bay Asian Local Development Corporation, a voluntary, non-profit organization pushing the interests of all Asians; and he had contacts with satellite informal leaders, individuals such as church leaders who provide leadership to segments of the population.[1]

Since the Cambodian group is small, the strategy has been to form alliances with other Asian groups for funding and to influence the course of local and municipal politics. The front leader, in this case the director just mentioned, recognizes that there are other, back leaders in the community who do not necessarily interact with the rest of the city.[2] The front leader joins ranks with the back leaders to get access to or votes from their constituencies.

There are some issues that engage the interests of one segment of the Asian-American population more than others. This is why various Asian groups have developed three strategies to deal with issues confronting their respective communities. Sometimes they go it alone. For example, the director of the CNG takes his case directly to the East Bay Forum on Refugee Affairs where he can air the concerns of the Cambodian refugee community. Sometimes a partial alliance is formed with other ethnic groups. This was the case when Laotians and Vietnamese in the East Bay Vietnamese Association and Cambodians formed an alliance to support a losing supervisorial candidate in San Leandro in 1988. At other times, they form a much larger coalition. This was the case when the leaders from all the Asian groups formed a coalition to help Elihu Harris win election as Mayor of Oakland.

The Latino community presents still another type of informal political organization. San Francisco's Latino Mission District, like the Asian community, is made up of several cultural segments, original Californios as well as old and new immigrants. Unlike Asians who may have difficulty communicating among themselves if they do not speak English, lack of English is not a handicap to Latino cooperation.

The Asian model, where representatives of each group tend to represent the membership, is not found in the Latino community. There is more fusion. The leadership structure of the informal parapolitical organization in the Latino community in San Francisco is made up of heads of formal and voluntary organizations. The leaders of the Mission Economic and Cultural Association (MECA) who organize the annual carnival, the festival of the Americas and the Cinco de Mayo festivities, the Mission Neighborhood Center, Women Initiatives for Self-Employment, members of the Chamber of Commerce, prominent businessmen, church leaders – all are part of a network that can be activated to advance the interests of the community.

While modes of organization of the informal leadership – especially in terms of its composition and the position of the leaders in the community – differ among the African-Americans, Latinos and Asians, the way they connect with municipal authorities varies less. The formal power structure sees them as competing interest groups.[3]

INFORMAL PARAPOLITICAL ORGANIZATIONS AND FORMAL SYSTEM

In a typical Oakland School Board race, one of the incumbent candidates was defeated and replaced by a newcomer. The reason for that defeat was the inability, failure or unwillingness of the incumbent to deal with the Progressive Senior Citizens on the issue of a site for a Senior Citizen Center, one of the old school dormitories. The incumbent is reported to have said that he tried and failed to obtain the site. The Progressive Senior Citizens found that response to be inadequate and organized a negative campaign which led to his defeat. This is a clear example where an informal organization targets a specific candidate for elective office and influences directly the election outcome.

This example also shows how the formal system is shaped by the informal system. Electoral campaigns organized by the formal system, whose outcome is intended for the management of the formal system, are heavily influenced by informal organizations. The informal system stands in between two formal processes. It helps produce the formal outcome.

The informal system has been a way either to integrate or to segregate the community. While one group may use it to propel forward its own ethnic or racial demands or preserve its own traditions, in West Oakland it has rather served for the improvement of whole neighborhoods. This is why informal parapolitical organizations have been able to accomplish so much.

Many of the people in the informal structure are spread across the political spectrum from very conservative to very liberal. The thing that brings them together is the concern for West Oakland. Recently, they have become extremely liberal in terms of demands for services, but not always agreeing on the services that are needed.

The major figure in the informal system in West Oakland has been a septuagenarian who has been an active member and leader of grassroots organizations ever since he migrated to Oakland in the 1940s. He has been on the Advisory Board of Community Development, the Mayor's representative on the Senior Citizens Council and Chairman of the Budget Committee for the Oakland School Board. He has been perceived by the community and outsiders as the unofficial or informal mayor of West Oakland. In the early 1990s, he was also the chairman of CERT (Citizen Emergency Relief Team), the newest and probably most dynamic of the informal organizations in West Oakland.

The 1989 Loma Prieta Earthquake was a catastrophe of major importance throughout the entire Bay Area. In West Oakland, the collapse of the Nimitz freeway provided the image with the greatest visual impact and the point where most people died. Damage was extensive throughout the neighborhood. Out of that evolved a group whose membership numbers from 200 to 700, with a hard core of probably 150, a group that has been extremely successful within the official political system and has developed its own sub-government structure. This success was helped by Mayor Lionel Wilson who early on was supportive of their concerns. The city manager showed up at one of CERT's meetings and the district supervisor came on a regular basis. CERT developed its own Transportation Committee which, after several confrontations with CalTrans (the California Department of Transportation), has now been involved in the routing of the new Nimitz freeway. It helped draw the outlines of the two alternative routes proposed. It has been influential, forcing the formal system to bend its views and demanding the production of a negotiated order. The chairman of that committee has been invited to internal CalTrans meetings and in meetings with CalTrans and the Southern Pacific Railway.

A second committee has become involved in the redevelopment effort, making itself the voice of the citizen in the redevelopment of West Oakland. A third committee is involved in education and the political dimension of the organization, and their accomplishments are rather impressive. Every community from Vallejo to San José has, in fact, passed a resolution supporting the community's demand that the freeway not be reconstructed on Cypress Street, a route that effectively bisected the community. The city of Oakland has put on record three major resolutions that support this effort. The congressman and the assembly person representing the area both indicated strong support for the concerns of the residents. The organization, despite its volunteer staff, has made itself a strong voice for the neighborhood.

The African-American church has had an enormous impact in several ways on the day-to-day operation of this informal para-political organization. The office of CERT is in the Bethlehem Lutheran Church, an integrated but predominantly African-American church. The board of directors of CERT has in its membership a number of prominent black preachers, strong church members. According to a knowledgeable informant, if the septua genarian mentioned above is the informal mayor, another lay member of CERT must be singled out as the informal political theoretician and strategist for the African-American church in West Oakland.

The church has provided the informal system with two important sources of support. One is their membership: members of the informal system are recruited from among the membership of the church, though not exclusively. Another is the support of their ministers, both of whom have served to give the organization even greater legitimacy in the eyes of the formal system. From their pulpit, they have also supported the efforts of CERT. Some of the Protestant Ministers and Catholic priests have also provided invaluable leadership. One of them was, in fact, a member of the Mayor's Earthquake Relief Committee and was able to help CERT in getting grants from the Mayor's Earthquake Relief Fund.

Partial formalization of the informal structure has come about as a result of formal funding. Informal organizations sometimes formalize their administrative structure for more efficiency and to be accountable to the formal system. A supervisor's wife who happened to be the president of the group Neighborhood Housing was influential in getting CERT a grant from the San Francisco Foundation. Other churches have provided small amounts of money and have let CERT use their names for whatever goodwill this might bring them in terms of finances. Within the informal power structure, however, the single greatest liability is the lack of paid staff.

There has been a partial formalization of CERT in that the grants have allowed them to hire an executive director and secretarial staff. The physical office was given by the church, and the leaders are all volunteers. The grant was obviously given to CERT because West Oakland was so heavily affected by the earthquake and the magnitude of that effect is still visible. The degree of citizen involvement shows the official structure that this work of reconstruction has to be carried out.

INFORMAL PARAPOLITICAL AND FORMAL VOLUNTARY ASSOCIATIONS

Three types of relations can be envisioned from an institutional standpoint. These relations can be dominant, dependent or interdependent.

The relation is dominant when the informal co-opts the formal to join its activities while maintaining its vision, procedures and goals. The formal voluntary association joins forces with the informal group in an action that it has not developed but is willing to support.

The Urban League has sometimes been connected to an informal group put together to solve a specific issue, for example the installation of a stop light at a particular corner. A group of people might come together for such a purpose, aided by informal leaders. As they discuss the matter among themselves, they may seek and enlist the help of the Urban League in identifying the people to talk to at City Hall or, if the power structure is not responsive to their request, they may use the Urban League motto or banner to do their picketing. This is an example of the informal getting support from a formal organization to fight against another formal organization to solve a problem identified by an informal group.

The relationship of the informal to the formal voluntary organization becomes dependent when the latter seeks and enlists the help of the former. A voluntary association may not have the resources to show that they actually have mass support on behalf of a specific demand or grievance so informal leaders are often contacted to bring the grassroots out for a public show of support. In this case the cause is not devised by the informal, but they endorse it because they see much good in it.

The relationship between the informals and the formal voluntary associations become interdependent when both identify the same problem and work jointly or separately with different strategies, and inform each other about their progress, with the goal of achieving the same end.

INFORMAL LEADERS

Being an informal leader is a way of appropriating power and of being influential in one's community. It gives the individual access to authority. The intermediary role of the informal leader is played out in three different ways: as a politician, as a broker or middleman, or as an administrator. The politician provides informal leadership to the community. The broker helps City Hall understand the needs of the community. The administrator seeks funds and develops programs that he or she may then administer.

Informal leaders must be seen as liaisons between the community and City Hall, as providers of insights when they are called on by City Hall, and as shapers of policy when their opinions are sought before policies are developed and implemented. The mayor recognizes the power of these leaders and seeks their help to propagandize projects or get votes in a campaign. The mayor sees them as each fulfilling different functions in the community, and in calling on them recognizes the power of each one of them. The relations between the mayor and the informal leaders is a two-way movement: they call on each other to achieve stated goals.

The connections of the mayor's office with informal leaders at the neighborhood level are multiplex.[4] These relationships of informal leaders to the mayor's office lead us to ponder a number of questions. To whom are they connected both in the mayor's office and the community? Are they acting to promote their self-interests, placing themselves ahead of their competitors and in a strategic position to grab a job in the formal sector? Do they solve problems that the city could not solve? Do they constitute a layer linking the neighborhood people to the mayor's office – that is, instead of going to see the mayor would a citizen elect to see them, believing that they have better access to the mayor's office?

It is obvious that the natural leader may not have the same influence over people outside his or her neighborhood. His contacts are limited to the people of his neighborhood and to other local leaders with whom he may collaborate or be in competition. His contact at City Hall may be directly with the mayor or with an influential person in that office. The network of contacts both horizontally and vertically is limited.

The position of informal leader may lead to a job in the formal or public sector. Being an informal leader makes the person more visible, leads to contacts with city officials, and reveals how much that individual may be needed by the urban political establishment. Informal leadership is established over time and is based on a relationship of trust and the knowledge that the neighborhood and City Hall gather about the leader. The informal leader is knowledgeable about the community and commands the support and respect of his followers.

Some informal leaders may decide not to take a formal government job because they realize how much influence and power they have as informal leaders. They hold their influence by virtue of knowing a lot of people, young and old. The fact that they are not paid helps project their image as people caring for the good of the community. What kinds of influence can informal leaders exert on City Hall, since they perform a self-appointed leadership role? Can co-optation lead to the incoherence of the informal organization? Informal leaders who have been co-opted cannot drop their informal role overnight. This is not a decision they can make by themselves – the people are also a factor in carrying out that decision. They will continue to call on them on informal group matters and problems. The other factor is that the positions they are given may be tied to their informal role in the community as a constituent basis of support. In that case, informal accessibility remains important in the performance of the new, formal job.

In the informal political arena, power is both dispersed and hierarchized. In the neighborhood, one must distinguish the center-state informal leaders and the satellite informal leaders. While the center-stagers provide leadership to the whole area, the satellites may do so only to their individual blocks. We see here the hierarchization of the leadership among informal leaders. The satellites refer individuals or inform the center-stagers about neighborhood problems to be addressed, or seek the advice of the center-stagers, or lobby the center-stagers to bring the problem to the attention of the other sub-groups or the general assembly. This can also be done by contacting directly the other informal leaders representing various micro-neighborhoods.

The informal leader can also be found in the person of a formal official who has left a formal job. There are cases of members of city councils who lose elections and return to the neighborhood. What does it take for such a person to become an informal leader? If he or she was an informal leader prior to landing the formal job and continued to maintain contacts thereafter, the re-entry will not cause any problem. People who were not formerly informal leaders can become leaders because of the expertise they are able to offer. To the extent that such formal leaders accept the role of informal leaders, they will be recognized as such by the group.

The informal organization is sometimes rife with division because of the ideological orientations or different perceptions of the informal leaders. The issues that tie the group together do not necessarily include the willingness to support any one individual informal leader for public office. One informant stated that many people like him as chairman of the transportation committee, but should he become a candidate for an elective office in the formal system they would probably oppose him because of feelings and personality clashes. He believes that people are afraid of him for the same reasons they like to have him available to fight the 'outsiders'.

The same qualities that make people into leaders in the informal sector may make it very difficult to get them accepted as part of the formal sector in anything other than an advisory capacity. The neighborhood did run Paul Cobb once for city council, but he lost to another candidate in a hotly contested election because the mayor threw his weight behind the other candidate. The informal sector did not have access to the major financial resources of the larger formal structure and could not muster its people power in a unified way against the incumbent.

In the mayoral campaign of 1990, the informal leaders of CERT were not able or were unwilling to consolidate their voices behind one candidate. In fact, the members of the board of directors supported the incumbent Mayor Lionel Wilson. The chairman supported Elihu Harris, and two others supported Wilson Riles. Harris won. Some see this lack of unanimity as a lack of unity of purpose, but others see it as a strategy to avoid having all their eggs in one basket.

MODES OF RELATIONS WITH THE FORMAL

From the standpoint of the informal, relations may sometimes be established with the formal system by means of co-optation. Co-optation can be seen as total or partial. It is total when an informal is given a job in the formal sector on a full-time basis so that his primary allegiance is seen to be shifting to the formal. It is partial when the informal is brought to the formal in an emergency or advisory capacity.

The participation of people in the formal sector tends to act as a barometer of the understanding of their impact on the informal sector. The degree to which a person is competent in the formal sector reflects his or her performance in the informal. Someone who lacks competence in the formal sector may lack credibility in the informal. The informal sector relies greatly on verbal interaction and the degree to which a person is able to articulate and to express himself with a certain vigor.

The formal sector selects advisors from the informal. The formal sector calls on them to help with matters concerning the informal and at the same time the informal advisors enhance their status in the informal setting. In this capacity, they help the informal community get grants and community services and ease the tension that the formal sector may experience in dealing with the informals.

The advisor serves as a paradiplomat representing the interests of the informals. The person from the formal sector calls on such expertise to help solve problems. The ties made here through the middleman-advisor strengthen the position of the informals.

The idea that the informals are a pole or the other side of the formal can be seen in two ways. Since members of the informal group may not be the same as those of the formal, they are linked to each other through the informal leaders, or the members of the formal group may be the same individuals who participate in the informal. They may be full-time participants in the formal and part-time participants in the informal.

The neighborhood informal organization has its own way of penetrating the formal political system. It does so through informal-to-formal contact by submitting and presenting issues; through informal-to-informal political processes at City Hall (kitchen cabinet); through informal-to-informal administrative processes; and through simultaneous multiple attacks in all three branches.

THE MAYOR'S OFFICE AND INFORMAL ORGANIZATIONS

The formal system is aware of the existence of the informal process: the actors are engaged in it for their political survival and maintain collaborative contacts with informal political leaders as part of city governance. Astute politicians sometimes come from the informal system and have been elected to office because of their grassroots connections. Once in office they continue to maintain these links. In fact, election does not mean that they give up their membership in those groups. They continue to play major roles, at times convincing the membership to support their policies. For example, they may need the grassroots to show up for a special meeting at City Hall to support a piece of legislation or to put pressure on the mayor and city council to favor a specific policy. Sometimes they simply feed the grassroots with inside information not available to other residents. Other politicians who might have been active in one grassroots area may develop cordial relations with other grassroots areas once they are elected. What Knoke (1990: 93) said about the leadership role in industry can be applied here as well: 'The most powerful actors are the incumbents simultaneously holding key positions within both webs of formal and informal relations to other organization participants.'

From the City Hall side, the elected officials see informal organizations as separate groups waging turf wars, challenging or supporting their candidates, but lacking in management, plans and an awareness of larger issues. They are seen as forming many factions throughout the city.

The strategy used by City Hall to reduce their influence or to control them is to create special citizen groups as a way of infiltrating and creating a balance to these opposition groups. Individuals may be co-opted to serve as interlocutors along with others from other competing groups. This way they do not represent a threat to unity and can bring forth issues that deserve the attention of the city as a whole.

City Hall recognizes that the informal system is very hard to manage. The city neutralizes troublemakers among the informal leaders in three major ways: (1) by harassment – that is undermining their leadership; (2) by ignoring them, or (3) by creating alternative informal leaders. The strategy has also been to create alternative informal groups that one can control, or to infiltrate and encadre informal groups with one's own people. As other informal leaders are created, they are made to play against each other. Troublemakers are ignored: their telephone calls are either not returned or are only returned one or two days later, and they are not invited to public social affairs.

From the city angle, the rulers look at the informal at the neighborhood level with an eye to co-optation and collaboration, to enhancing the positions of allies and downgrading the positions of hostile informal organizations, and to a combined strategy based on the importance of informal organizations linked to unions, their size, age, fragility and their overall importance in the neighborhood.

From the city side, two kinds of informal groups can be distinguished: the neighborhood groups and the corporate world. The corporate world is made up of the old-guard businessmen, lawyers, professional people and old families who are entrenched in city politics. Behind the scenes, they make decisions and influence the policy-making process and policy implementation. They call council members, sometimes meet with them, and because of their ability to provide services to elected officials (such as raising money for an election or giving financial contributions to a campaign) their voices are heard.

The formal sector establishes its own informal apparatus for efficiency in handling issues, to serve as links, or to listen to informal groups and bring their demands to the attention of the mayor. Telephone conversations prior to a meeting provide an informal way to get votes and solve the problem of split votes. This informal procedure is necessary for efficiency because meetings cannot last long enough to work out all the details in a particular matter. The issue may be well discussed informally ahead of time because this cannot be achieved in a two-hour meeting.

The informal players at City Hall are the formal employees. These are the loyalists who comprise the kitchen cabinet of the mayor, protect him or her and prepare policies. The center of the administrative process is identified as the gang (administrative decisions are made by the gang); political policies and planning rest with the political clique, but political decisions are made by the gang.

The informal sector in the mayor's office consists of his staff. If one cannot see the mayor, one may be able to see members of his or her staff. The mayor may listen more to one staff member than to another. There is a hierarchy both in the way the mayor perceives the neighborhood-based informal groups and the way he perceives the informals in his office. In the neighborhood, one's position depends on one's importance and loyalty to the mayor's office. In the office, it is based on friendship, whether one knows the players, and whether one can provide reliable advice and loyalty.

The informal group, which is informal by definition, is asked to present formal demands to be discussed formally. Both entry and influence can be informal, using an informal approach to deal with the formal politician, their informal organization and the formal bureaucracy with its informal apparatus. This is why, for analytical reasons, it is productive to separate the formal political system from the formal bureaucratic system, although in practice they are intertwined and interdependent.

The formal administrative process creates its own informal administrative structure. The bureaucratic process with its own rigidity is an obstacle to efficiency. It operates both formally with outsiders and informally with insiders. To cut through the bureaucratic process, informal leaders who have contacts in the office can penetrate the informal bureaucratic system to achieve a formal outcome. Sometimes the informal group at the neighborhood level is able to adjust to the informal political process at City Hall and not to its attendant informal administrative process.

THE INFORMALITY OF URBAN POLITICS

The informal dimension is ever more present in the organization of urban politics at both the neighborhood and city government levels (Guest and Oropesa, 1986). That informality is part and parcel of the formal political system in the running of the everyday affairs of the city, in the electoral process, in the policy environment and implementation, and in the overall relation of elected officials with their constituencies.

Urban politics is played out on two registers: the formal that is legal, visible and official, and the informal that is hidden and sometimes illegal. Because of the top-down nature of administration, a vast array of human activities is not accounted for although they play key roles in the conduct of the political life of the city. The informal register gives sustained life to the formal system.

Urban politics has an informal dimension because of the web of informal relations the elected officials carry with them. The network of informal relations that they have prior to coming to the city office and the informal ways they have been socialized to do things cannot be dismissed overnight. In fact, they must rely on some of them to survive in office. The notion of 'kitchen cabinet' certainly implies that even within a formal cabinet there may be a clique closer to the boss who influence the direction of urban politics.

The informal arena is the place where political maneuvers that cannot be carried out in the open are accomplished. Informality provides a back-up to speed up cumbersome procedures, to reduce the time that cannot be saved and to do things that cannot necessarily be done in the open because doing them openly either defeats the purpose or is illegal.

Informality and formality are two sides of the same political process and reflect the sociological reality of everyday life. In the conduct of urban affairs, informality comes to the rescue of the formal system, while the formal is used to give legitimacy to the informal. In other words, the formal system and process of urban politics cannot be understood fully without paying attention to the informality that it contains and that shapes its content.

THE POLITICS OF INFORMALITY

The informal political process exists in every American city for the simple reason that democracy allows it, the imperfection of the formal governmental system invites it, neighborhood residents welcome the opportunity to make their voices heard in an effort to improve local conditions, and city officials routinely use it to achieve a successful outcome to their activities.

The politics of informality can be characterized as providing the formal system with an arena of activities that it uses and is forced to react to. I have investigated six domains worth examining: for face-saving, for problem-solving, as a safety valve, as a back-stage rehearsal, as an information system and as a plateau of resistance.

The informal is used by the formal in matters of face-saving. An individual in a given situation can shift from formal to informal as a way of diffusing tension and getting smoothly out of a situation that could be embarrassing. It is basically a survival device.

The informal is also an arena where problems initiated in the formal domain may find their resolution. The informal domain is able to resolve problems efficiently because illegal, unethical and otherwise secret deals can be done there. Often the US Congress is divided on an issue, which means that the formal system cannot solve the issue or could do so only with more time. After adjourning the session, the legislators are able to make informal deals with one another in the corridors, in the cafeteria or on the tennis court. Once this is accomplished in the informal domain, they can come back to the Chamber and take the votes. This is a clear case of the informal rescuing the formal.

The informal can also be seen as a safety valve. When everything else has been tried, the informal may be sought as an ultimate arena. It allows a decontraction of the formal system by way of its expansion.

The informal system provides a back-stage rehearsal. It is here that compromises are made, the problems of the formal are contemplated and strategies for change are developed. That rehearsal predicts the possibility for success in the formal, visible on-stage performance.

The informal also provides a system of communication to the formal. Such informal communication gives access to information not otherwise available and is an informal system because of the informal acquisition, analysis and content of the information. Few local and city politicians could survive without being fed routinely with this kind of informal information.

Informality also allows a route to opposing a leader or the operation of the formal system. It is in this arena that much consciousness raising and strategies of protest are developed. It provides a forum where true feelings can be unveiled, secrecy can be kept and an alternative political morality can prevail.

The politics of informality has its own intentionality and goal: to enhance one's own status, to prevent an opponent's ascension or to defeat an enemy, to speed up an administrative action, to exploit all possible sources of information, to keep alive important connections or to advance a common cause.

FORMAL LEADERSHIP AND INFORMALITY

To strengthen our argument for the role of informal practices in formal political life, we cannot rely exclusively on the relations between the grassroots and the mayor's office in their expression through the informal political and administrative process. Another crucial test is to show that even the relations between city officials and state or federal officials are mediated by informal practices. One would expect that the relations between these entities ought to be formal. This is not always the case. The formal apparatus comes in merely to rubber stamp what was already gained or solved in the informal domain.

The mayor's web of informal relations connects not only with the local urban electorate but also with officials at the state and federal levels. The latter are the ones who help the city secure state and federal monies for the mayor's constituencies. Becquart-Leclercq (1978: 261) notes that 'to activate such power resources mayors must develop a personal relationship network that opens routes for groping their way through the tangled web of state agencies and for facilitating requests that may be blocked in administrative labyrinths.'

The elected mayor may have no alternative other than to use these covert processes. They are so much entrenched in the way that formal politics function that it would be disadvantageous to a city if the elected officials were not to get involved in them. Becquart-Leclercq (1978: 254) puts it rightly when she notes that 'municipal leaders are therefore confronted with this dilemma: play a game of covert relationships or handicap your community.' She further notes that, unlike the French situation where informal contacts with the higher echelons are the primary locus of informal activities, in the American case the informal relations tend to be more intense between the mayor's office and the local community (Becquart-Leclercq, 1988: 131).

The informal relations have their own rituals operating under the stamp of secrecy. Becquart-Leclercq (1978: 262), who studied the French system of networks linking mayors to prefects, has identified some of its characteristics. It tends to be 'face to face, and personal ... activated by telephone calls, personal visits, luncheon invitation – never by letters'. These are all modes of contact that nurture and reinforce the informality of the relationships. These patterns of behavior transform the formal into the informal. They have been a transformative characteristic. Once the ritual is accomplished, the relations can become informal. They serve as a medium for the expression of informal relationships.

These informal relations must be seen as an exchange mechanism, one that maintains a balance favorable to both parties. It gives the mayor access to power resources, speeds up the bureaucratic process and the delivery of goods (money), and strengthens his or her position in the city, providing an advantageous broker position *vis-à-vis* other cities. At the same time, it provides a constituency for the state or federal elected official or support for state or federal policies. To the extent that each one receives something in return, the relations may be stable over time (see also Becquart-Leclercq, 1978: 262).

In a formal system that is supposed to be run by formal rules and procedures, the informal network 'perverts relationships between rulers and ruled, thwarts collective expression of demands, handicaps participation and leads to favoritism' (Becquart-Leclercq, 1978: 280). Through its perversion, this practice leads necessarily to nepotism because it positions some individuals in a better position than others, it discourages some from using the formal process, and discriminates against those who do. These practices help build a hidden stratification system and can blur the policy of fairness, leading to an apportionment of state services on a basis other than equality and contributing to the reproduction of inequality in the process of state allocation of resources. The mayor is then to the state official what the grassroots leader is to the mayor – that is, part of a circle of protégées working for their own benefits and those of their constituencies. Those mayors who are able to establish and maintain sustained informal relationships with state and federal leaders are likely to gain more for their communities than those who do not.

These informal relations show the subtle ways informality interfaces and interferes with formal practices, and so influences them. The success of the mayor in getting the money from the state cannot be explained exclusively in formal terms. One sees here the intermingling of both informal and formal in the production of the formal outcome. Informality provides a political space in which at the same time to deroute and to reroute the formal process. (Derouting means going over a threshold to analyze and disarticulate an aspect of the formal process. Rerouting means going back over the threshold and returning to the formal with a formalization of the informal content.) The formal political process is thus fraught with informality. Behind the formal façade, there is a benign discourse and practice of inequality and discrimination nurtured by the web of informal political relationships.

THE PROCESSUALITY OF INFORMAL POLITICAL PRACTICES

Through the decoding of informal political practices, we can see political informality as being processual and also multivocal. Processuality refers to its content, its backward and forward linkage with the formal sector and its transformation.

The informal system is processual because it is constantly in the making and remaking. This process can be activated for various reasons, among them being changes in goal-orientation, in the actors themselves, in the content of the network of relationships, in internal forces (internal transformation) or in external forces (generated by a varying amount of external constraints).

The informal system is also processual in a more lineal fashion in terms of its historicity. It has its beginning in establishing a hidden agenda or in a period of formation. This corresponds to the slippage from formal to informal. It has a peak which corresponds to the periods of analysis, maneuvers, deals and informal decisions. The third phase is that of re-entering or the formalization of the informal outcome. Each one of these phases corresponds to moments of inverted informal to formal relationships.

The informal is also processual because it shapes the formal system. Processuality here means two things: the informal is adjusted to the ways of the formal, or may be on its way to becoming formalized. Its interdependence with the formal system is the cornerstone of its processuality.

Notes

1.   There are various sites of power where the informal raw politics is cooked, practised and channelled into the arena where the formal political system can interface with it and sometimes recoup it. We have found that the Chinese, Filipinos, Laotians, Cambodians and

Vietnamese have their own separate organizations where local issues that affect their ethnic groups are discussed. They form an Asian alliance for the purpose of funding and politicking, especially in their interface with state and city agencies. However, the ethnic politicians identify themselves not as representing their specific ethnic groups, but rather the larger Asian community. The East Bay Asian Local Development Corporation provides them with a front region for the expression of their public discourse.

2. The informal leadership is subdivided into front region and back region leaders. The back region leaders join ranks with the front leaders for the purpose of making their voices heard and achieving their goals.

3. For a historical analysis of the participation of ethnic minorities in the formal political system in San Francisco, see Wirt (1974: 240–71). On African-Americans' and Hispanics' attempts to shape the formal political system in Oakland, see Hayes (1972) and Browning et al. (1984).

4. The relations between grassroots leaders and the mayor's office are understood here in terms of exchange theory (Lomnitz, 1988; Blau, 1964) and patron–client relationships (Knoke, 1990).

5

Informality, Interstitiality and the Modern Firm

The formal firm is one arena where formality is supposed to reign supreme because it is organized according to a rational blueprint to enhance its effectiveness. The formal organizational chart identifies the positions to be filled by employees and establishes the formal rules for dispute resolution and for conducting daily and routine business within the firm. Yet it would be wrong to believe that any of the formal firms in the San Francisco Bay Area operates on the basis of formality alone. As we will see later, informality is also part of the formal operation of the modern firm.

There is a tradition in the sociological literature that explains the existence of informal practices in the firm in two ways: either as preceding the formation of the formal firm or as being produced by the formal firm. In reality, these two explanations complement each other. The argument for the precedence of informal organizations is explained by way of locating the issue in two structurally different positions. For Etzioni (1970: 216) the preparation of a blueprint to set the goals and operation of the organization is certainly drawn up by a small group of people through informal interactions and it is through those informal practices that staff and their positions in the firm are discussed and other practical matters are decided. Simon (1966: 148) pushes the argument even further by locating the issue not only prior to the preparation of the blueprint and after it is agreed upon, but also before the firm starts to run smoothly. He refers to the role of the 'initial shake-down cruise' to give the first operational boost to the organization. He sees the fulfillment of the relational aspect as a necessary step for each employee who joins the firm. The newcomer must develop informal relations with the people before being accepted fully by the group. Informal organization

103

is seen as the engine for the establishment and the functioning of the formal firm. Barnard (1958: 120), using a similar line of argument, remarks that 'formal organizations arise out of informal organizations.'

Informality in the firm is also seen as a consequence or a production of formality. It is so because formality has its own limits and does not cover all aspects of the operation of the firm and also because human beings always find ways to circumvent imposed structures that restrict their freedom of action. Informality is produced by formality to prevent any stalemate in the operation of the formal firm. In this light, Barnard (1958: 120) notes that 'when formal organizations come into operation, they create and require informal organizations'.

Johnston (1956: 25) argues that it is the inability of the firm to meet the needs of the individuals that leads them to create informal organizations.[1] He notes that 'informal organization will arise in many cases in order to compensate for the deficiencies in the formal organization.' The informal organization, far from impeding the firm, actually helps it achieve its goals and evidently helps the individuals to satisfy their needs.

Ever since the 1920s there has been an interest in studying various aspects of informal organizations in formal organizations. Early on it was clear that there are an enormous number of informal activities going on within the modern firm. These studies were undertaken to show the existence of informal organizations in formal organizations and the functioning of specific informal entities like the grapevine (Davis, 1953; Sutton and Porter, 1968) and the clique system (Sayles, 1966), the relations between formal and informal organizations (Barnard, 1958), and the importance of informal organizations in the running of formal organizations (Roethlisberger and Dickson, 1947).

The various studies on informal organizations have been couched in the functional mode of analysis.[2] Blau (1964: 271) tends to reinforce that trend by calling for 'a functional analysis of the informal organization which explores the distinctive functions of the informal group structure in a bureaucracy'. What is sought here is a description of the contribution of the informal organization to formal organization.

The functions of informal organizations in formal organizations are spelled out in the research literature in terms of meeting the needs of three different entities: to meet the needs of the individual participant, of the clique or the group, and of the formal organization. Barnard (1958: 122) underlines the rationale of the functional argument by making a case for the importance of understanding the role or impact of informal organizations on formal organizations. He sees their function as being 'that of communication ... that of the maintenance of cohesiveness in formal organizations ... [and] the maintenance of the feeling of personal integrity, of self-respect, of independent choice.' Summarizing the extensive literature on informal organizations, Iannaccone (1964: 223) stipulates that they are either seen 'as primarily subversive ... as a healthy supplement to the formal organization ... or as providing for the psychological welfare of organization members'.

Other researchers pinpoint rather the limits that formal organizations put on the performance of informal organizations. In this top-down approach, Dalton (1959: 237) tends to stress the restrictions of the formai system on informal organizations. He notes that 'first, the formal largely orders the direction the informal takes. Second, it consequently shapes the character of defenses created by the informal. And third, ... it requires overt conformity to its precepts.' Although one recognizes the need for the formal system to regulate the spread of informal organizations so that they do not become too cumbersome for the operation of the formal organization, it is an exaggeration to believe that 'the formal structure performs no function unless it actually sets limits to the informal relations that are permitted to develop within it' (Simon, 1966: 149).

That informal organizations exist in formal organizations is beyond any doubt and therefore is not a point of controversy (Selznick, 1964; Britan and Cohen, 1980). What is not so clear is the multiple ways in which the informal organization is related to the formal organization and the nature of these relationships.

The goal of this chapter is to show the way in which informal organizations serve as a foundational basis to formal organizations. By stressing the interstitial aspects of the relations between the formal and informal organizations. We will see why and how 'beneath the formal organization and obscured in part by it, there lies a "real" world consisting of the way things get done and how people truly behave in organization' (Iannaccone, 1964: 223). To accomplish that goal, we will study the interstitial position of informality in the modern firm. As the underside of the formal firm, the manifestation of informality will be seen as a process and also as an enclave. As an enclave it develops a niche within the formal firm, and, as we will see, the way it is connected to the firm has ramifications that can have an impact on the firm. As a process, it fills the interstices of the operation of the formal firm.

INFORMALITY AND HIRING PROCEDURES

'Last year, we were hiring someone in the firm. There were quite a few good candidates around here and from out of state. We read their applications including their vitaes and statements of interest. And we decided to invite some of them for an interview so that we could get to know them and they would have an opportunity to visit the place and meet with some of us. The selection process was complex because they were for the most part competent people with a lot of experiences and strong letters of recommendation. I was particularly drawn to two of the applicants because I know the people who wrote their letters of recommendation. These are individuals for whom I have a lot of respect.

'Not all the individuals who applied for the job had done so because they had heard that there was a job opening in our firm. Actually we did contact some people and invited them to apply either because we knew of their work or because friends had suggested that we got in contact with them.

'There were a couple of incidents before we made the final decision. For example, three people called to provide us with background information on specific applicants. Much of it was gossip and could not be verified easily. There was a specific individual we were interested in hiring. However, someone informed us that she had heard that the applicant had had a problem with a woman in the firm where he was working. We contacted one manager who knew our applicant and he did corroborate this piece of gossip. Despite his formal and outstanding credentials, we ended up hiring another person on the basis of that confidential piece of information given to us over the phone.'

In the hiring process the interstices of the formal procedure can be seen to be filled with informality. Hiring means three things: search, rejection and selection. Although formal notices are published listing the qualifications of the person to be hired or giving a description of the job, there are informal ways to invite specific prospective employees to apply. These individuals are identified on the basis of their contacts or friendships with certain persons. These behind-the-scene maneuvers are discriminatory, and sometimes illegal if done openly, but are allowed to survive because they are done covertly. They already influence the nature and the content of the next step, the rejection of unwanted candidates.

Informality rules completely in the rejection process, partly because of the informal bias in the search itself. Some will be rejected because of a lack of contacts. Others will be rejected because it is presumed that they will not fit well with the informal life of the firm, including its conflicting cliques. Others will be rejected because of informal criteria – often unspoken but nevertheless real – such as ethnicity, gender or sexual orientation.

The selection itself is fraught with informality. The candidate is seldom selected on the basis of competence and experience alone. Informal inquiries are made about his life in general and responses are not contained in the letters of reference, but rather are conveyed through telephone calls and informal talks with other people who may know the candidate. But often, there is a *godfather* who is pushing the case because the candidate is a friend of a friend, because it is presumed that the candidate will join *my* little clique or is likely to support *my* views, or the candidate graduated from *my* alma mater or belongs to the same church or club that I am a member of. These informal criteria fundamentally influence the formal character and the outcome of the hiring process in the modern firm.

The informal criteria can either help to strengthen or weaken the formal criteria, and thereby enhance or undermine the ability of an individual to land the job. They are part of the hiring process and cannot be dismissed as being non-existent. In fact, because they provide a context in which to understand the formal criteria, they can influence the process so much that they can shift the decision one way or another.

INFORMAL LEARNING AND TRAINING

Formal training is not sufficient for survival in a firm. It provides information on the technical and professional aspects of the job, but in the everyday operation of the firm, even some of these technical aspects are learned through the informal routine. This is so because formal training covers only the expected, not the unexpected.

Informal training is routinely done on the job. The information a clerk or secretary needs may not be available through the formal channels. For example, the new employee who comes in wants to know or find out who is important and who is not, the power behind the scene, as a way of playing a fair game both in the formal and informal sectors. There is informal traditional knowledge or a tradition of informal practices in every firm that he or she may want to get acquainted with: which people do not get along, what conversation is anathema because of past experience, the way of doing things that reflects the group culture. This is part of the informal training that enhances a new employee's ability to relate to both the formal and informal aspects of the corporation.

Informal training is achieved through the apparatus of informal learning. Informal learning is part of one's daily life in the firm and does not entail any specific requirements. In this light, one may justly argue that 'Informal learning is embedded in everyday life, taking place consciously or unconsciously. For such learning to take place, no prescribed setting, schedule, topic, centralized focus and institutional structures are necessary' (Akinnaso, 1992: 78).

Informal learning is essential for survival and a successful career in a firm and it is the way in which practical knowledge is acquired. Practical knowledge which enlightens everyday practice must be distinguished from specialized knowledge. For Akinnaso (1992: 82) notes: 'practical knowledge is not a secret form of knowledge but, rather, one that members of a given society normally share equally … Specialized knowledge, on the other hand, is normally transmitted in institutions through formal learning.'

INFORMAL COMMUNICATION

'In this firm, management did not want to give him a permanent position and at the same time did not want to fire him for monetary and legal reasons. A secretary who had typed a confidential memo started spreading the news around. Management had made a final decision about him, but did not want to make it official. A gossiper informed him about this bad news. Knowing that there was no support from the top and to prevent more damage to his reputation from the negative gossip that was going around, he left the firm.'

'A secretary typed an evaluation that was supposed to be confidential about a white woman who was dating a black man. The secretary was all over the place telling people that this woman was not going to be promoted to partnership in the firm. Since she had learned the bad news from the grapevine before she learned it from the boss, she got herself ready for a confrontation with him. The manager was caught unprepared when she confronted him. She was able to save her job.'

'A manager was dating one of the female employees. She told a friend of mine that I was going to be transferred to another department. When that happened, I was not emotionally disturbed because I had learned from the grapevine the reasons for my transfer. Actually the formal letter of transfer did not spell out the reasons for the transfer. If it were not for the information I learned from the grapevine, I would have probably left the firm.'

'I was working as a teller in a bank. At that time the policy of
the bank was that employees could not date each other. One
could go to lunch with a friend, but no dating was allowed on
the premises. You know, there was this young and charming
man who was interested in me. We did not show any sign of
affection for each other in public. However, gossip about our
discreet affair took over and finally reached the manager of the
bank. Management stepped in and transferred one of us to
another branch of the bank.'

In the everyday operation of the firm, there are two overlap-
ping systems of communication. One is formal and used and
understood by everyone in the firm. It is supposed to be the
main channel of communication for the transmission of
information both vertically and horizontally among the
employees of the corporation. However, it is not the only form
of communication available to employees. To the formal one
may add the informal system that feeds the formal, complements it, explains it, and comes to its rescue when it fails in
its transmission process.

The informal system conveys both important and casual information. Any information that can affect the well-being or the job
of an employee is accepted as important. Casual information
refers to communication on the routine operation of the firm that
keeps one abreast of what is going on.

The informal communication system in the firm is itself subdivided into two categories, or has two aspects that are also over-
lapping: informal communication and the grapevine. Although
they are different from the formal communication system, they
are nevertheless not identical even though they belong to the
same universe.

We find these categories in the interstices and they are central
to the operation of the firm. In distinguishing the two aspects of
the informal communication system, Alexander (1974: 89) notes
that the first is related to the physical proximity of workers in the
same firm and 'is directed toward filling their work-oriented
information needs'. This is different from the grapevine or rumor
which 'arises from the deep-seated need of each employee to
know what is happening in his environment'.

For Simon (1966) such informal communication comes about because individual goals may be different from the organization's goals. The informal communication is used as a way of reaffirming the self *vis-à-vis* the structural constraints of formal organization. Informal communication provides a corridor where the actors can psychologically detach themselves from the organization, exchange information among themselves, and reflect on their behavior and goals.

To understand the role of informal communication in the firm's communication system, it is important to keep in mind three things: the direction of communication (Blocker and Schauer, 1965), the content of that communication, and its negative or positive influence on the operation of the firm. Communication is a key factor in the running of the firm because it links people to each other and messages are given for the coordination of the operation. However, formal communication alone is insufficient to do the job. There is a hidden dimension that complements formal communication – this is informal communication. Sometimes it reinforces, contradicts, complements or simply shapes the content of formal communication. The total communication of the firm comprises both the formal and informal aspects.

The formal communication pattern does not capture the totality of messages diffused within the organization. The informal communication pattern is also important in that it provides a parallel system of diffusion: it takes the information from the formal sector and distributes it to the informal group, and it takes information from the informal and distributes it to the formal. In its role, it reproduces the maintenance of the group. Gossip is the mechanism that maintains the group, that protects individuals in the group, and that provides information the individual needs for his adaptation to the firm.

There are many things that cannot be said formally because they would be inappropriate, or cannot be said to everyone because they would be seen as unethical. Informal communication provides an alternative route for face-to-face, personal relations. In this sense, it cannot be superseded by the formal communication system.

Zey-Ferrell (1979: 224) distinguishes two directions in business communication, through the 'horizontal' and 'vertical networks'.

The horizontal network is 'between persons on the same level in a given department or between different departments'. The vertical network which comprises both upward and downward communication is found 'between persons at different ranks in the same hierarchical level and between different hierarchical levels'.

The grapevine is packed differently depending on the listening audience. The communicator passes on information to protect and enhance his or her interests. The multivocality or difference in the content of the grapevine may be due to these different packagings undertaken by the initiator. The gossiper provides information tailored to the needs of his or her audience. The listener may change the content also, but this is a different issue.

In a firm, gossip may not be exclusively a face-to-face enterprise. The telephone is often used for that purpose because it transcends spatial boundaries and even allows more opportunities. A secretary who is busy may not have time to visit a friend on another floor, but through the telephone she can reach that person without leaving her office.

At the port of Oakland, a good deal of informal communication goes on. By telephone, gossip travels from the port to the main office in downtown Oakland. Sometimes someone from the port goes to the main office and passes on news, believing that it is new information. However, a telephone call had preceded him and turned it into old information.

Gossipers feed the group with information supposedly limited to management, and alert people to issues under discussion, decisions taken, or individuals to be fired or hired. What was to be secret is revealed and may cause embarrassment to management and the people concerned.

Managers are not immune to gossip. They enter it horizontally through informal communication with their peers for various reasons, whether to be informed of what others think or simply as an efficient procedure to accomplish things in a speedy manner. It is also used to channel information down to and receive feedback from subordinates. Some even use the network to carve a power niche for themselves. Gouldner (1954: 92) notes that:

Strategic replacement enables the new manager to form a new informal social circle, which revolves about himself and strengthens his status. It provides him with a new two-way communication network; on the one hand, carrying up news and information that the formal channels exclude; on the other hand, carrying down the meaning or 'spirit' of the successor's policies and orders.

Gossipers also report to and feed management. As a source of information, gossip may influence and help management to shape its formal policies or decisions. For Simon (1966), 'The grapevine is valuable as a barometer of "public opinion" in the organization. If the administrator listens to it, it apprises him of the topics that are subjects of interest to organization members, and their attitudes toward these topics.'

Management uses informal communication as a trial balloon to prepare people ahead of time, to test people's reactions, and to get feedback before a formal decision is taken. Management also uses it among peers to speed up processes. Issues are discussed informally over the telephone, at the tennis court or in the cafeteria to reach consensus prior to formal meetings.

Gossip is also used by management as a way of testing the ground before firing someone. Such gossip emanates from higher up. Sometimes the content of gossip goes around and the person concerned is the last to know. In any case, it often prepares the person for the forthcoming bad news. At the same time, it gives management enough time to evaluate the reactions of the group and to prepare the final order. If the reactions are too strong, management may back off or prepare ways to circumvent foreseeable problems. If there is no negative reaction, then management can proceed with the final decision.

It is also used by employees as a weapon to retrieve information from management. A false rumor is spread and management comes in to clarify wrong rumors. Thus management is forced to provide information that it would not otherwise have provided.

Gossip may serve as a corollary to formal communication by providing additional information or an exegesis of the rationale or even the interpretation of what was said. In any case, it provides explanation that allows one to make better sense of the formal communication. Zey-Ferrell (1979: 234) notes that 'informal communication networks ... may clarify, elaborate, and add new meanings to otherwise confusing or uninformative messages from the superordinates. They may provide the necessary rationale for imminent changes in the policies and procedures of an organization.' The supplementary role played by the grapevine *vis-à-vis* formal communication has also been stressed. Indeed, Davis (1953: 44) notes that 'often formal communication is simply used to confirm or to expand what has already been communicated by grapevine.'

In any firm, there are individuals who are central in the diffusion and creation of informal knowledge. They are the most knowledgeable about the daily routines of the firm. They go out of their way to seek new information, provide their own interpretation of this informal information, cook it, and seek out people with whom to share this information. Their clients are superordinates who are interested in knowing what goes on among employees, peers who want to be informed about management views, and subordinates who regard such information as a form of protection. Such individuals become specialists in informal knowledge communication and diffusion, and people turn to them for information.

These specialists link together all the facets of the operation. Some people derive a feeling of power from gathering and diffusing information, so making others dependent on them. This is especially the case of those who have access to confidential information and who initiate the gossip. For some it is feedback information that is provided while for others it is new information or an interpretation of something that is already known. In both cases, the rumor diffuser uses his position as a source of power that can be manipulated to enhance his status. It is his ability to control this knowledge, to diffuse it on his own terms to those he selects, that constitutes his power and makes him stand apart from others.

In the logic of this analysis, one can see the secretary in a firm as an informal intelligence agent. Having access to confidential knowledge, she can pass on information to upgrade the status of one colleague and refuse to share the same with another to undermine his position. Having access to knowledge from different sources, she is in a position to assess or evaluate that knowledge to protect a friendly boss or to downgrade the status of an opponent. She has some control over the flow, content and direction of this informal information.

Managers devise various ways to create niches for the expression of cooked informality. My claim is that informality is sought in some circumstances by the managing staff for the purposes of better communication. To the formal lunch meeting one may contrast the informal ones. Informal lunch meetings are sought or organized for the purpose of providing information, explanation about formal communication, or to retrieve information that could not be secured otherwise.

These informal meetings provide management with a feedback system and a way of understanding constituency and representation and of evaluating the unseen or the hidden dimension of people's behavior. They allow management to hear new ideas or to be re-educated in ways of doing things more efficiently.

These informal meetings decrease frustration in that they promote understanding and dialogue. What is incomprehensible can become understood. People may influence the executive, causing management to change their minds if the information is given in a non-threatening way.

These informal communication meetings tend also to socialize people in the culture of the corporation. One person may lead the conversation in an area where other people are not knowledgeable and sometimes not interested. They foster not only upward/ downward informal dialogue but also horizontal dialogue among peers.

One manager in San Francisco informed me how informal communication among employees led to a change in policy. Various employees had discussed among themselves the need for a retirement plan, and this information was brought by someone to management. At a shareholders meeting, the issue was discussed formally and a resolution to establish a plan was passed. This is a clear example of informal communication influencing the formal corporation.

A major characteristic of informal communication is that it is verbal, travels fast from mouth to mouth, and also has its pitfalls. Davis (1953: 44) finds it to be 'highly selective and discriminating'. It spreads rumor, half-truths and is prone to deformation as it makes its way from the communicator through the various listeners in the chain. These rumors, depending on their content, the network covered and the intention of those who propagate them, can do a good deal of harm and lower the morale of co-workers. They can thus have a negative impact on the firm.

There is also a time factor that helps us to understand the intensity and density of informal communication. At some periods gossip activities are more intense than at others: when a company is not doing well, when the possibility for a merger is being discussed, when the company hires new employees or is about to fire others. These are circumstances that tend to feed the circulation of gossip.

INFORMAL LEADERS AND THE CLIQUE SYSTEM

'People were whispering around saying that John [not his real name] has too many colds. From the wordprocessing department where I worked I went to the copymachine area and everyone was asking the same question. Do you think that John has AIDS? It was in the early 1980s and everyone was afraid of being in the same room with someone with AIDS. A group of us talked to Joe [not his real name] and asked him to inform management that we are upset about John's presence in the firm. Once management learned that John had AIDS, a public health person was invited to meet with us and John was placed on disability leave. He died shortly thereafter.'

The modern firm relies on both formal and informal leaders for its operation. Informal leadership is found at various levels among the executives, middle range management and the employees, depending on the size of the corporation.[3] The informal leader is the person people turn to for help and to assess everyday life in the firm. Just as there is usually more than one clique within an organization, there may be more than one informal leader.

For Sayles (1966: 91), the leader fulfills important functions in his relations with his followers. For example, 'he initiates action, he facilitates a consensus and he provides a link or liaison with the outside world.'

When there are various cliques vying for membership and power within an organization, the role of the leader may well include the protection of the group. Roethlisberger and Dickson (1947: 380) refer to informal leaders 'who took upon themselves the responsibility of seeing that the members of a group clung together and protected themselves from representatives of other groups within the company who could interfere with their affairs.'

Because of the level of education and individualism of the American worker, the informal clique system provides a safety valve for improving the firm, for criticizing the firm, for standing up for one's rights, for learning about the organization of the firm, for inquiring about others (intelligence gathering), for protecting the firm from bankruptcy, for the maintenance of morale in the firm and for improving the employee's psychological satisfaction.

The informal leader is a focus for conflict resolution with management. Sometimes the informal leader brings up the issue and the employees come to support him. Sometimes the group has a conflict with management and elect an informal leader to represent them.

Although the informal leader is supposed to represent the interests of all the workers in his clique, sometimes there is segmentation based on gender and ethnicity. Within the firm, there may be subgroups with their own informal leaders based on people sharing the same ideological, business or political orientation, gender or ethnicity.

The informal clique system is important in the decision-making process in the firm. At the level of management, one can judge their importance in two ways. The informal clique is often able to reach a consensus on issues before attending a meeting. They present their points more clearly, are better prepared than others, provide the best argument, and get decisions passed according to their will. In this case, the clique is able to manipulate the rest of the group.

Sometimes an issue is brought inadvertently to a meeting. The clique has not discussed it beforehand and, as expected, no consensus and no decision is reached. Once consensus is later sought and achieved in the informal sector, the clique is able to return to the formal meeting room for a formal decision.

INFORMALITY AND GENDER AND ETHNIC DISCRIMINATION

The modern firm provides us with an arena where we can study and analyze how informality produces gender and ethnic discrimination.[4] Formal practices are the realm where all the members are invited to participate. These are open practices that allow the flow of communication, socialization and the daily operation of the firm to proceed. If these formal practices are not discriminatory by design, one may conclude that ethnic and gender discrimination does not exist in the firm. In fact it may well do so, and the study of informality provides a route by which we may understand how its existence in the informal practices colors or sexualizes formal practices.

The hiring of minorities and women helps alleviate the physical and visible characteristics of discrimination but does not eliminate them. This policy may bring about formal harmony in that a *modus vivendi* may be reached in the formal apparatus, but it also may create informal disharmony.

In the firm, the formal visible system is the public arena where a drama is unfolded. The presentation of the self in public may or may not coincide with the private self. If the motivation of the firm lies within the informal organization, we find that people are often excluded from participating in these influential informal organizations on the basis of ethnicity or gender.

Decisions concerning the orientation of the firm may be made through the informal channel by individual managers who play tennis together, who meet informally for lunch or who call each other on the telephone to discuss informally forthcoming formal business matters. This is the way intelligence is shared, policies are discussed and decisions are made. The formal meetings are held simply to rubber stamp what was already decided by a few through informal means. A member of a minority or a woman

who is not invited to play tennis cannot prove that there is discrimination, but in fact there is and the script is hidden. This
explains the frequent frustration of women and minority members who are part of an executive committee and who find themselves alone when voicing an issue. Decisions are made through
the informal clique on Saturday morning on the tennis court or in
the men's locker room, and they were not invited to attend – in
fact, they were excluded.

This type of discrimination cooked out of informal practices
would be less damaging if it did not have any effects on individual careers. Just as informal practices enhance career promotions
for those included in the right circles, they are a handicap or
obstacle to career advancement for those who are excluded.
Knoke (1990: 103), corroborating a point made earlier by Kanter
(1977: 206–42), notes:

> ... how structures of informal communication limit women's
> and minorities' access to critical information and experiences
> essential for career development. Old-boy networks still flour-
> ish in business, government, and academic organizations,
> giving differential advantages to the protégés of established
> executives, bureaucrats, and professors in the scramble for
> preferred positions.

Such practices also show the limits of formal regulation and
legislation. They address only the formal aspects of society, not
the informal ones. Legislation can force a firm to hire women and
ethnic minorities at the managerial level, but cannot force male
managers to invite them to their informal gathering where they
may talk informally about formal business matters or where they
may engineer important decisions to be ratified later in formal
business meetings.

THE GRAMMAR OF THE INTERSTITIALITY OF INFORMALITY

The informal system is interstitial in that it is part of the formal
system. An interstitial system may not have a life of its own. Its

life depends on its interdependence with the formal system, on its interaction with the formal system, on actors who belong to the formal system, and on an outcome that may facilitate or hinder any action undertaken in the formal system.

As an interstitial system, it splits a formal process into two units, stands in between and links one to the other. It is able to accomplish this because it receives its impetus from the former. It decomposes, deconstructs unblocks and provides the means to recompose the formal system. As a transitional process defined by its interstitial characteristics, it influences the trajectory of the formal system.

As an interstitial system, the informal system informalizes aspects of the formal system by inducing formal actors to be informal in their behavior, to engage in informal activities, to use temporarily the formal space informally, or to transform the formal space into an informal space.

As an interstitial system it is absorbed by the formal system. Thus actions taken by the informal system are absorbed into the formal to allow the formal to proceed and move forward. These interstitial practices become part of the working of the formal system.

As an interstitial system, it does not intervene in each step taken by the formal system. However, the possibility is there to reconstitute itself for one or more events and to disintegrate temporarily until a need is felt for it to reappear.

The system is considered to be interstitial when the actors become interstitial to conduct an activity, when the activity or event is interstitial, when the outcome is interstitial, or when the network is either interstitial or mixed.

The interstitiality of the informal system is characterized through its main features as being essential, necessary or transitional. The interstitial system is *transitional* when it allows the formal system to pass from one state to another or from one situation to another. It becomes *essential* when this interstitiality becomes a *sine qua non* in the functioning of the formal system. It is *necessary* when it becomes the best avenue to speed up a process that allows the smooth operation of the formal system.

Notes

1. Johnston (1956; 6) has found that there exist three basic types of informal organization. He characterizes them as 'informal social organization', 'informal subversive organization' and 'informal supporting organization'.
2. Merton (1961: 112), following the same Durkheimian predicament, finds 'informal social structures as mediating between the individual and large organizations'.
3. In the formal firm, we find a proliferation of microsites of informal power (raw and cooked) along vertical and horizontal lines that at times undermine, rearrange, influence or reinforce the formal site of power. Knoke (1990: 93) notes that 'the informal communication relations continually generate and modify the distribution of legitimate authority among persons and groups inside organizations'.
4. To understand how informal communication among the majority group affects the position of the minority group in the firm, see Fairhurst and Snavely (1983).

6

Informality and Urban Medical Practices

In the San Francisco-Oakland Metropolitan Area, informal medical practices exist side by side with the formal medical system. In fact, it is possible to misunderstand the relations of the residents to the formal system of medical care if one does not take into consideration the reality of informal health and medical practices. Informal medical practices show up at the level of understanding of the causes of illness (lay logic), diagnostics (the folk medical realm to which the illness belongs), the search for an appropriate form of healing (self-care, spiritual or folk healing, the hospital or private clinic), and the implementation of the regimen (the extent to which the patient follows the recommendation of the medical doctor to the letter, accepts the spirit of the recommendation, or else rejects it altogether). There is another arena where informal medical practices could be studied here – that of the hospital as a bureaucracy in terms of informal networking among staff, the spread of gossip, the reality of informal communication and the clique system. Since some of these issues were discussed in the context of the modern firm, we will not pursue them vigorously here. Let us concentrate rather on other aspects of the formal–informal relations in medicine so as to show how informal health and medical practices serve as a support to the formal system.

Without focusing on the literature pertaining to the working of the modern hospital system, it is fitting to review briefly that aspect of it that serves as background to the issue at hand. Informal practices are located in various positions in the health care system. They are found among patients, at the staff level and in the working of the insurance policy delivery system.

It has been argued that informal practice is a key element in the success of medical doctors because it affects assignment, referrals and indirectly the size of one's clientele. Hall (1946:

31), who had earlier interviewed a number of physicians in New York, notes, for example, that 'the allocation of positions in the institutions, the pace at which one receives promotions, the extent to which one has patients referred to him, all hinge on the workings of the informal organization'. There are no clear rules that govern these transactions. Much depends on patronage and sponsorship. The young doctor who becomes the protégé of an older physician or a clique is in a more advantageous position for advancement and upward mobility than those who do not have such a back-up.

To complement Hall's analysis, which implies the existence of a fraternity who may hold down those its members fail to support, Freidson argues – without presenting data to support his claim – that 'there can be numerous "fraternities" in a single community, and there are certainly numerous "fraternities" in the profession as a whole ... These colleague groups are built up by the mechanisms of patronage and boycott; and, by the very consequences of the mechanisms themselves, they must be fairly well segregated from each other' (Freidson, 1988: 194). In his speculative argument, Freidson sees informal practice as the basis for the formation and split of fraternities or the informal clique ('the old-boy network'), the means by which people are recruited into these groups, and the basis for their survival and reproduction over time. Although hidden, these mechanisms provide clues to understanding the make-up, competition and conflict among these informal medical cliques or fraternities. Two Bay Area physicians who were interviewed confirm Freidson's observations through their own experiences.

The existence of informal practices is also acknowledged and taken into consideration in the delivery of insurance policies. Graham (1985: 47) notes that 'private insurance is expressly designed for medical care, not health care: it meets the costs of surgical and pharmacological repair but not the costs of full convalescence.' Informal health care provided at home by members of the family, which is important for the total recovery of the patient, is not covered by insurance. One sees here the relations of the formal medical system to the insurance industry and indirectly the recognition of the informal sector as a support system to the formal sector.

In our understanding of society, social scientists have developed theoretical models to understand the structure of formal systems. Even when informal systems come into the picture, they tend to be studied from the standpoint of the formal social systems. In other words, the logic of the formal systems is used to make sense of the informal systems. I intend to continue to reverse the strategy. The focus is not on how formal systems help us to understand informal systems, but rather on how informal practices help us to understand the formal health and medical system. Informal systems have their own rationale, and constantly adjust to and help shape the structure of formal systems.

Often formal systems function smoothly and become productive because of their interactions with informal systems. Formal systems cannot even be fully understood without seeing their links with informal systems, and informal systems themselves cannot be studied as isolated enclaves. They are culturally, symbolically and structurally connected to formal systems.

In this chapter, we will examine one aspect of the theoretical problem concerning the links of the informal system with the formal system. Although the formal system might be studied as a support system to the informal system, we prefer to reverse the strategy once more by looking at how the informal system can be a support system. In so doing, we are not denying the 'relative autonomy' of the formal system; rather the informal system serves as a back-up or support system to the formal system.

INFORMAL MEDICAL PRACTICES

'I always have some basic medicines in the house. Last month, my daughter was coughing: I gave her some cough medicine, aspirin, hot teas with honey and a lot of orange juice. Since she did recover after a few days, I did not have to take her to the clinic.'

It is a general observation that there are many folk medical practices within the minority ethnic communities. It is often said that the main reason why people do not attend hospitals when they are sick is poverty.[1] In fact, this is only one among other reasons.

Across the board, rich and poor alike in the San Francisco Bay Area are involved in informal medical practices.

General opinion associates the formal with the mainstream Anglo population and the informal with the minorities. This is not true: the Anglos have their own informal practices and the informal category embraces all segments of the population.

Some illnesses belong exclusively to the domain of folk practices. Illnesses like *susto* (fright) among Mexican-Americans in the Mission District are treated only by folk remedies.[2] Interaction of the patient with modern medicine through a medical doctor in private practice or through the general hospital comes about only as an ultimate recourse.

In the general population, people do not necessarily see a physician every time they feel pain. Here again they tend to take care of themselves and if the pain continues they may decide to see a physician. For common illnesses like colds, people do not routinely see their doctors, but simply take care of themselves. What this amounts to is that folk medical practices are widespread across the various social classes.

To show the magnitude of informal medical practices as performed in private homes, Levin and Idler (1981: 64) identify:

... the two most frequent sources of sickness and death in this society, the ubiquitous minor illnesses and injuries of daily life: common colds and flu, indigestion, skin conditions, household accidents. The other major source of morbidity is chronic disease, which can vary in severity from hay fever to diabetes to cancer. These two types constitute by far the greatest proportion of disease in most people's lives, and they are precisely the diseases which are cared for, best and most often, by the family.

On the one hand we have a formal system of medical care that does not cover all the health problems of the city. On the other hand, we have a number of health problems that never reach the formal medical care system. These problems are solved through the informal system.

In a sense one may say that the informal system is an extension of the formal system because it solves health problems that might otherwise reach the formal system, but in addition the problems it cannot solve are referred to the formal system for their resolution. From the patient's standpoint, formal and informal medical systems are two poles that complement each other.

THE INFORMAL REFERRAL SYSTEM

'When I came here from New York, I did not know a lot of people. I had a health problem and I needed to see a doctor. I talked to two employees at the workplace. One did not like any of the doctors she was seeing at the HMO. The other told me about an older doctor who has a very good reputation in town. She said to me if you want more information about him you can call my girlfriend. I did talk to her girlfriend who also recommended him to me. I went to see him and he has been my doctor for the past ten years.'

Freidson (1961) found that prior to seeing a physician or to visiting a hospital, the client may depend on an elaborate informal referral system. This preliminary period covers the practices of informal health care experimentation and informal acquisition of knowledge. Many health problems are solved at this level because personal experimentation has been successful or the information acquired through the informal network has helped cure the illness.

Freidson (1961) speaks of the lay referral system in contrast to the professional referral system. In my judgment, it is more accurate to speak of the informal referral system in the sense that it may include aspects or actors from the professional system. For Freidson (1961: 18) the lay referral system can be very elaborate in that:

The process of seeking health began with purely personal, tentative self-diagnosis that implied their self-administered treatments. Upon failure of these first prescriptions, members of the household were consulted. Aid in self-diagnosis was sometimes sought from laymen outside the household – friends, neighbors, relatives, fellow-workers, a former nurse, or someone with the same trouble. Indeed, when exploration of diagnosis was drawn out and not stopped early by cessation of symptoms or immediate recourse to a physician, the prospective patient referred himself, or was referred, through a hierarchy of consultant positions. The hierarchy ran from the intimate and informal confines of the family through successively less intimate lay consultants until the professional was finally reached.

In deconstructing the lay referral system, Freidson (1961: 146) identifies 'the lay referral structure [which] is a network of referrals in that consultants not only diagnose and prescribe but also make referrals'.

The focus on the informal referral system is important as it helps to show how the informal system is a support system provided in three ways. First, it keeps individuals from using the formal system when they can solve their health problems by themselves and in this sense prevents the formal system from being overburdened by unnecessary treatment procedures. Second, it provides a filter for the transition to the formal system. When the problem reaches the formal system, it is likely that some informal medical practices have been used. Third, it allows the patient to be more receptive to modern medicine because informal practices were helpful not in curing an illness, but in leading the patient to modern medicine. In consequence, modern medicine concentrates on those illnesses that folk practices cannot cure.

Because there is a body of illness that never reaches the hospital, the study of health care cannot concentrate exclusively on the formal system which may not account for informal practices. The focus on the informal referral system allows us an opportunity to see what is hidden behind the formal system of medical care.

Although the focus on the lay referral system has helped clarify aspects of medical practice, 'this concept [was not introduced] to understand the structure and organization of the informal health service' (Graham, 1985: 31). We must pay attention as well to the internal dynamics of informal medical practices.

ILLNESSES, SELF-CARE AND HOUSEHOLD-HEALERS

'My mother is the one who cares for us when we are sick. She lives not far from here. Even though I am now married, whenever my mother comes to the house if one of my children is sick, she always prepares something for the child: tea, vasoline if it is a cut and so on. She used to make my father, younger brother and two sisters drink all kinds of teas when we were living in Louisiana. I am not into that kind of stuff. From time to time, I do simple things for my children when they have, for example, bad colds.'

It is a truism to say that there are folk and non-folk illnesses that are cured outside of mainstream medicine. Each individual has his own list of illnesses and symptoms that can be treated through self-care or with the help of lay people. Sometimes these lists are shaped by one's socialization in an ethnic group.[3]

Each ethnic community has its healers, the most common among them being family members like the mother who has learned the medical knowledge from an older generation and who is able to use it to cure members of the family. Self-care is an informal way of taking care of one's self and has no cultural or class boundary in that it is done by everyone in society.

What these scattered medical practices do is to relieve the formal system form the burden of a tremendous number of health problems that never show up at the hospital. The informal system supports the formal by sparing it a number of cases. These cases will not appear in the statistics of the formal system. Because of these informal practices, the hospitals and physicians can concentrate on more severe cases and sicker patients.

Informal practices are reproduced over time through the socialization of people into them, sometimes extending the size of the population which uses these practices as the information is shared with others.

Because these informal practices often actually cure people, they return healthy people to work in the formal system of society. In a sense, they appropriate the role of the hospital. At the same time, these informal practices help produce a segmented market for health care. Competition occurs in one area of that market.

The informal medical system also provides an alternative avenue for illnesses that cannot be treated by the formal system of medical care. Then, the latter serves only as a last resort. The informal treatment allows formal patients a psychological relief in the knowledge that they have tried everything to secure health.

Such treatment provides an opportunity for less orthodox medicine to be practised. It supports the formal system in two ways. On the one hand, at the beginning of the illness, folk remedies are tried and if not successful, the next step is taken: the use of modern medicine. On the other hand, if modern medicine cannot solve the problem, then folk remedy is the last resort.

This last resort strategy shows the limits of formal medicine. In this light, one may say that folk medicine rescues the formal medical system when there are more than just physical aspects to health care.

WOMEN AS INFORMAL HEALTH CARE PROVIDERS

When we introduce the notion of gender and focus on the home front, it becomes evident and even central that women play a major role in this informal arena. Health care is not only provided at the hospital or the private clinic, but also at home. This informal aspect can be best studied at the home level. The decision to seek professional help is often taken after the home trial and experiments had failed. The home is an informal laboratory where folk remedies are tried, where informal knowledge is shared and informal therapies are experimented. As Sharma (1992: 59) notes, 'studies of lay health practices in Britain have shown that women take major responsibility for the health care administered informally through the household.' In the various ethnic communities in the San Francisco Bay Area, we have found that the mother plays a central role in the early diagnosis and treatment of sickness in the other members of the household.

The focus on home health care forces us to recognize the importance of women in carrying out much of this service. It is the woman as wife and mother who more often than not cares for the rest of the family. Thus, it is right to say that 'informal health care has remained part of the domestic economy' (Graham, 1985: 25).

In providing home care, women also serve as mediators and negotiators linking the domestic to the public sphere. Graham (1985: 26) writes that 'their caring role places them at the interface between the family and the state, as the go-betweens linking the informal health care system with the formal apparatus of the welfare states.'

In this same light, Sharma (1992: 63) speaks of 'the cultural "micro-climate" of the household' in matters pertaining to informal health care practices. Thus it is important to explain how the household provides a niche for these informal practices and the organizational mechanisms that sustain their survival and reproduction.

SUPPORT SYSTEM

When we speak of the informal system as a support system, we imply a certain degree of dominance and hierarchy, and of course the existence of a formal system. We imply a normative stance in that the formal is central and the informal is peripheral. We imply that by focusing, on the informal we will understand what kind of contribution it offers to the maintenance of the formal system. We finally imply that the existence of the informal may depend in part on the existence of and relationship with the formal.

In studying an informal system such as folk medical practice and its relation to a formal system such as modern medicine, one may be able to illustrate empirically the process that I have in mind. Folk medicine functions as a back-up system in regard to modern medicine, and by back-up system, we mean three different things here.

First, it is a *complementary system* in that it is a specialized system that intervenes for specific health problems that fall in its domain. The complementary role of folk medical practices which serve as a support system to the formal system is manifest at various levels. At the treatment level, sick people use folk remedies to cure their ailment. Those remedies vary from one ethnic group to another because of different cultural backgrounds.

Second, it is a *sustainable system* in that it helps unclog the formal system so that it can operate smoothly, so that the informal system serves as a dumping ground for the formal system. By serving as a safety valve to the practitioners of modern medicine, it alleviates the burden of formal medicine and indirectly sustains it.

Third, it is a *feeding system* in that it provides remedies and techniques that are gathered and used by the modern system, that is it transmits to the formal system cures that are formalized into pharmaceutical drugs, and patients for whom it has no cure. There is a constant movement of people from folk practices to formal practices.

While modern medicine concentrates on its own rational domain, folk medicine fills the cracks for common and folk illnesses for which modern medicine has not yet found remedies.

We acknowledge that the informal system has a much more important role in the functioning of society than has been recognized by social scientists. It allows the formal system to operate in its own domain. It also allows the formal system to return to the informal system things that the formal system cannot resolve or accommodate. There are two processes here: one is the solution that the informal system provides which could not be provided by the formal system. The second is the removal of the action from the formal to the informal system, thereby freeing the formal system to concentrate on things that it can do or deliver. This safety valve function allows users of the formal system an alternative means: that of using the informal system for specific endeavors.

As a support system, the informal medical system performs a series of functions pertaining to the well-being of the formal system, the users of the formal system, the users of the informal system, and the well-being of the informal system. It is a support system in that it spares the formal system certain tasks, allowing it to continue to seek solutions for the problems for which it currently has no solution to offer. It also allows the formal system the possibility of either ignoring or pushing to the cultural margins of society certain items which might fall under its domain.

The smooth functioning of the formal system depends on the existence of the informal system. The formal system must be defined in terms of its differences from the informal system, that is the parameters of its objective boundaries. In its intentionality, the formal system does not operate without its recognition of the existence of the informal system, for some of the reasons previously mentioned.

The users of the formal system also take advantage of the informal system. They function in the formal system to the extent that this system can help them take care of all their needs. However, any deficiency either perceived or real in the formal system may lead them to seek solace in the informal system.

The users of the informal medical system also recognize the existence of the formal system and use it when it is to their own advantage. They understand that the informal system also has its own boundaries. Problems that they cannot solve from their participation in the informal system are brought to the formal system to be solved there. They develop classificatory themes to distinguish what belongs to the formal system from what belongs to the informal system, and it is from that frame of reference they decide when and how to move from one system to the other.

The users of modern medicine have access to and utilize the folk system of health care. They are socialized in their own cultures to distinguish illnesses that belong to the domain of modern medicine from those that belong to the domain of folk medicine. They may further distinguish illnesses in terms of their natural, spiritual and magical origins and select the modes of treatment and the healer as a function of those categories.

The informal system functions smoothly depending on the state of the formal system and the capacity of the formal system to meet its own needs. This may explain why the boundaries of the informal system may expand or contract. When the formal system is unable to accommodate its users, the informal system tends to expand; when the formal system expands its boundaries, the informal system's sphere of activity tends to be reduced.

The expansion of the use of folk medicine by users of modern medicine is related to the inability of the latter to reach out to or accommodate everyone in a given community. When modern medicine is unable to cure illnesses among its consumers, these individuals end up enlarging the group of folk medical users. They reach out or resort to folk medicine in search of efficient remedies.

In contrast, when practitioners of modern medicine make an aggressive effort to make themselves and modern medicine available to the community, as has happened in socialist Cuba, the sphere of activity of folk medicine is curtailed. In other Caribbean islands, where budget cuts have forced hospitals to close their doors, folk medicine continues to flourish and has enlarged its domain of action. In the Bay Area, folk medical practices are used extensively among undocumented immigrants who, because of their legal status, are afraid to use the facilities of the modern hospital.

THE EXPANSION OF THE INFORMAL SYSTEM

One of the functions of the informal system as a support system is its ability to expand itself, taking over tasks that normally fall under the aegis of the formal system. That expansion is caused and can be explained in a number of ways. It is not the result of internal forces, but rather of external circumstances.

The sphere of activity of the informal system may be reduced because of decisions taken by the formal sector to reduce consciously the size of the informal sector or its sphere of activity. The reasons for such a move may come from a perception that the informal system plays a negative role that must be curtailed, that it impinges on the formal sector's sphere of activity, or simply as a result of the expansion of the sphere of activity of the formal system.

In contrast, an expansion of the sphere of activity of the informal system may come about as the result of the reduction of the sphere of activity of the formal system, users' demands, its ability to attract participants or the legitimacy factor.

The informal system sustains the formal system through its trajectory, its growth and contraction and its ability to provide a back-up to the users of the formal system. Its structure varies in relation to the behavior of the formal system. This leads us to look at the impact of the status of the informal system as support system on the formal system.

STRUCTURING OF THE INFORMAL SYSTEM AS SUPPORT SYSTEM

Because of its status as a support system, the structuring of the informal system places some limitations on its development and internal organization. It functions mostly as a response to events over which it has no control. The dependence of the informal system on the formal system becomes a reality that it cannot overcome.

For that reason, it has no hold over the actor-participants. Many are not full-time participants in the informal sector; they simply fall from the formal sector. The users may even move to the formal sector depending on what this sector can offer, its availability and the willingness of the actors.

The internal structuring and articulation of the informal system has its own dynamic which is itself influenced by the ability of the system to expand or reduce itself. Expansion may increase the multivocality of the system while contraction may decrease its level of complexity.

As a support system, the informal system resolves its internal crisis or conflict in two ways. One is simply to achieve some form of *modus vivendi* within its sphere of influence. The other is to serve as an exit mechanism to allow the sufferer to seek a solution in the formal sector. In such a case, instead of serving as a support system, it becomes a burden to the formal system. This constitutes the negative aspect of that functional characteristic of the informal system. One may say that it provides both an 'exit channel' to solve problems emerging within its domain of action and an 'entrance channel' to solve problems arising from within the domain of the formal sector. It is functionally indispensable to the formal system.

As long as folk medicine provides an alternative to mainstream medicine users, it plays a positive role. However, it also may be seen as a burden when health problems remain too long within the folk medicine domain before they are brought to the attention of mainstream practitioners. A simple health problem that could be treated easily by modern medicine can, under such circumstances, become a complex medical problem that can be life-threatening.

The internal structuring of the informal system must also be seen in terms of processual flow. It constantly adapts itself to external realities while maintaining its internal rationale. It continues to evolve and to re-adjust itself. The positive aspect of its support may derive from its structural linkages with the formal system.

CORE AND PERIPHERY

Like the formal system, the informal system is divided into a core and a periphery. That segmentation affects the informal system in two major ways. One concerns the relations between the center and periphery in the formal system and the center and periphery in the informal system. The other concerns center–periphery relations within the informal system.

It seems a paradox to say that the informal system tends to display a higher level of formalization at its core than at its periphery, but that is indeed the case. The core tends to represent what is central, ideas to which the majority of practitioners subscribe, a structure of action to which most adhere. The periphery refers to the marginal, minority practices and practices that are somewhat different from those in the core. However, the process by which the periphery may coalesce into the center is similar to what can be observed in the formal system.

The relations between the center of the formal system and the center of the informal system do not necessarily represent harmony of interest. They represent different practices at two extreme poles, but are seen by users as complementary. Peripheries in both systems may present a less antagonistic outlook. While the center in the informal system uses either the periphery or the center of the formal system in the same way as the center and the periphery of the formal system uses the center of the informal system, it is often the case that the periphery of the informal system will first use the center of the informal system before moving to the formal system.

The core–periphery distinction is an important one in the study of the informal system as a support system. It shows that the support system is not an undifferentiated one, but rather has its own poles of action. It also reveals that the informal system is not monolithic, but rather provides an array of alternatives to the users of the formal system, formed into a hierarchy according to the internal logic of the informal system. It reveals that the informal system is made up of a series of poles that act as centers out of which radiate peripheral entities enmeshed in complex networks of relationships.

CRISIS AND CHANGE

All social systems are susceptible to crisis and change; none can be conceived of as static. This is why the relations between the formal and the informal system must be seen in terms of processual flows. How, then, does the informal system handle internally or externally propelled crises?

The formal status of the informal system is not necessarily permanent. Over time, actors may move to the strict realm of the formal system. They are not confined to the informal system. The informal system is constantly decomposing and recomposing itself, losing old users and incorporating new ones. This is one of the basic tenets of change and evolution in the informal system. In addition, part of the informal system may be taken over *in toto* by the formal system. On the other hand, the informal system may also attain the status of a formal system, which occurs when the formal system is pushed to the margins and is replaced by the former informal system.

CODE SWITCHING

The support system notion does not imply that the two systems are similar or follow the same logic – this is not the case. For that matter, it is necessary to point out that the movement from one system to another implies a process of code switching, by which we mean here the ability of an individual to move from a system that operates on a given set of rules to another that operates on a different set of rules. We are not concerned with the outcome that is supposed to be the same in both situations, but rather with questions of procedure and rationale.

The code switching mechanism infers not the uniqueness of each system, but rather the flexibility of individual actors to adapt to them. This is one formal structural link between both systems and actualizes the reality of the informal system as a support system to the formal system.

Notes

1. For an elaborate presentation of this argument, see Bullough and Bullough (1972).
2. For an analysis of folk concepts of illness and disease among Mexican-Americans, see Schreiber and Homiak (1981).
3. Home treatment in the Chinese community in San Francisco is widely practised. On Chinese-Americans' use of the informal health care system, see, for example, Gould-Martin and Ngin (1981).

7

The Informal Arena of Inter-Ethnic Relations

Much of the sociological and anthropological literature on inter-ethnic relations tends to focus on the formal aspects of the interaction because of the prevalent assumption in the western world that society is run formally.[1] Informality is understood mostly in terms of personal preference and individual motivation, but not as a consequence of structural imbalance resulting from the asymmetry of structural relations and hegemonic practices.

To redress this bias in the focus of research, this chapter makes an attempt at delineating the mechanisms in the informal arena that may foster or hinder harmonious formal ethnic relations. We present the informal arena as a source of harmony or tension for the purpose of the argument so as to show that its study is central to any understanding of the working of inter-ethnic relations within the confines of the American city. It is a hidden reservoir or laboratory where ideas are tested, contested, reinvigorated or abandoned – ideas that directly affect behavior in any inter-ethnic interaction. The main question that is before us and that we will try to answer is how informal ethnic practices effect, positively or negatively, inter-ethnic relations in the formal arena.

POWER AND INFORMALITY

The notion of informality is at the very center of the locus of the encounter between the mainstream culture and the minority sub-culture in their formal and informal manifestations. At the center of this interface between formality and informality is a site of power that provides the rules for the articulation of the dominant system with the subjugated subsystem. It is then accurate to say that informal practices are centered around and shaped by the technology of power.

It is my contention that the disjunction between the mainstream-majority cultural practices and the minority subculture is reproduced in the modern city because of a power conflict, the manifestation of which we shall see later.[2] Power is the single most important variable that defines the locus of formality, not necessarily demographic size: there are countries where a small elite dominate a large mass, as in South Africa.

Power is the criterion that defines what is formal and distinguishes it from what is informal. Power is exerted to determine who is in and who is out and is also used to block some people's access to mainstream resources. This is achieved by various precarious and discriminatory rules and means that the mainstream system develops and controls. This use of power also undermines the ability of minorities to compete fairly in society and helps to control ethnic minorities through a number of practices and mechanisms ranging from symbolic coercion (ideology) through the bureaucratic apparatus (legal framework) to physical force (overt or hidden security forces).

For this reason, the phenomenon of ethnogenesis cannot be seen simply and exclusively as located in the colonial era, a production of the interaction between European colonizers and the colonized. It must be seen also as a production of postcolonial, industrial and postindustrial societies. To study its production is not enough; one must also pay attention to the technology of its reproduction.

DISSECTING THE MAINSTREAM SYSTEM AND MINORITY SUBSYSTEMS

The American city is made up of a mainstream formal system fed by subcultural systems, some of them ethnicity based. The mainstream system is made up of a formal system and an informal subsystem that either precedes or is produced by the formal system. Ethnic minorities participate in the mainstream formal system but also have their informal subsystems, which are influenced by the dominant system. Actually some of these are sometimes formal minority systems colonized or dubbed informal by the mainstream system. The mainstream system functions on the basis of formal practices that are shaped by two divergent sets of informal rules: those of the mainstream and those of the ethnic minorities. What we call informal rules in the majority system are often formal rules internal to the system, but which have been peripheralized by the majority system on rational grounds. What we call informal rules in the minority system are external to the majority system and occupy a site that is exploited by or sometimes used against the formal system.

In their participation in the mainstream system, members of ethnic minorities find themselves at a disadvantage on different fronts and at different levels. It is worthwhile identifying the locations of their disadvantage. The focus on informal systems allows us to see such disparities.

Minorities are at a disadvantage while participating in the formal system of the mainstream because they must obey rules that they may not have helped to create. The democratic process does not work to the advantage of many minorities because they may operate on different cultural assumptions and are engaged in different cultural practices. Conversely, democracy favors the mainstream actors more than the minorities because of their familiarity with and socialization in such a system.

The minorities are at a disadvantage because they lack power and access to resources through which they could effect changes. In fact change, in many cases, can occur only if the majority system allows it to happen. Thus it will be change tailored or coached by the majority. This is so because any prospect for change initiated by the minorities is likely to be taken over by the majority system or must be formulated in such a way as to meet the democratic criteria and rationale acceptable to the mainstream. (Of course, we are not referring here to revolutionary change or to collective protest undertaken by members of ethnic minorities to enhance group status or to achieve self-determination.)

Many members of minorities are handicapped by their own previous socialization in minority families and communities and the background they carry with them in their interaction with the formal system. Thus they may find themselves alien to the

mainstream both because the formal rules of operation are constantly undermined by the informal practices of the mainstream
in which they may not be invited to participate and by their own
informal practices that may heighten the consciousness of their
differences with the formal cultural practices of the mainstream.

When the minorities join the formal system of the mainstream,
they expose themselves to further brainwashing and resocializa-
tion, but at the same time continue to carry the minority stigma
with them, as symbolized by their physical appearance which
cannot be hidden. Minorities are at a disadvantage because,
although formally welcome in the mainstream, they are not in
fact accepted as equal and therefore not always welcome in the
informal realm of the mainstream, the realm of power behind the
official scene. They may or may not be members of the mainstream informal network where real power is exerted. The mainstream informal arena constitutes one tangible locus – one where
power play is rehearsed – that contributes to the minoritization
process of ethnic groups and that makes possible the repetitive
process of the reproduction of ethnogenesis. Some aspects of the
behavioral expression of this process are delineated below
through the laws of 'similarity' and 'avoidance' on the one hand,
and the laws of 'sponsorship' and 'credit transfer' on the other.

LAWS OF 'SIMILARITY' AND 'AVOIDANCE'

The symbolic interactionist approach developed by Goffman and
others has been a source of inspiration to me and has led to my
formulating a set of laws that attempt to shed some light on the
mechanisms of the formality–informality articulation. By *law of
similarity* we mean that the mainstream system finds it more con-
venient to deal with people from the mainstream system than
with people from a different cultural system or subsystem: the
rules – both formal and informal – are understood by all concerned as a result of their socialization in the same culture. The
closer the minority subculture is to the mainstream, the more harmonious the interaction is likely to be. The farther away, the less
likely, because of a cultural disjuncture in the hidden, informal
arena. This is the primary rule that allows us to understand the

interaction between actors belonging to different ethnic groups. However, there are mitigating factors and circumstances that may facilitate or induce a smooth interaction.

Case 1. An Anglo immigrant couple living in San Francisco told me why they hired a white woman to care for their two-year old boy: 'When we were looking for a babysitter, we evaluated all the ethnic possibilities and concluded that it was best for us and the child to hire a white nanny. We wanted the boy to be raised as an American child and we felt that we would be more comfortable with a white nanny than with someone with a different ethnic background. We more or less assumed that she knew what we wanted and we had a general sense of what she could deliver. We could not assume these unspoken things if we had hired a Chinese or Chicano person.'

The *law of similarity* tends to come into play both at the informal and at the formal levels: our formal behaviors are shaped by institutional rules and formal conventions. In a formal setting, individuals tend to make an effort to be congenial and convivial, whether by their own inclination or because of institutional needs. At the informal level, there is less institutional but more group pressure to get along because of personal preference or motivation. Ethnicity then becomes a marker that shapes informal grouping and the grammatical rules of inter-ethnic interaction.

The *law of avoidance* states that whenever there is a choice an individual will be more likely or naturally to interact informally with a person of similar background and ethnicity and indirectly avoid an individual with a different ethnicity and culture.

Case 2. At a fund-raising social function in the basement of a church in the Bay Area, I observed the behaviors of some of the members of the group. While standing with a drink in their hands and socializing, people were engaged in conversation with whoever happened to be next to them. As they were invited to sit and eat dinner, ethnic clusters became more visible in the room. I jokingly asked a Mexican-American acquaintance why do all of you sit around the same table. She replied:

'We want to enjoy our dinner. We can speak Spanish if we want to and talk about things that are of concern to us. We just want to relax. If we were to go there [pointing to a table with white guests] we will have to be more formal in our conversation.'

Avoidance is more marked in informal than in formal settings because there is less personal freedom and more pressure to conform at the formal level. Avoidance can be 'benign', as one follows a personal preference based on compatibility, or can be 'aggressive' as when avoidance is based on racism – that is, an individual deliberately ignores the presence of another person because he or she belongs to a different ethnic group.

Avoidance based on ethnic preference is discriminatory: it separates people who belong to different ethnic groups from each other and at the same time allows the organization of informal grouping on the basis of ethnicity.

LAWS OF 'SPONSORSHIP' AND 'CREDIT TRANSFER'

The law of sponsorship sheds light on the acceptability of minorities by mainstream institutions while that of credit transfer sheds light on the acceptability of mainstreamers by minority institutions. By 'law of sponsorship' we mean that a member of a minority group is more likely to be accepted by a mainstream institution if sponsored by a member of the mainstream group than if he or she is not. Sponsorship provides a route for entry into the mainstream without breaking down the majority/minority dichotomy.

Case 3. An African-American professional told me that he was able to land his job because of the old-boy network. A white manager for whom he worked when he was a graduate student not only sent a strong letter of recommendation on his behalf but also, upon hearing that he was on the shortlist, placed a strategic call to someone he knew in the firm. According to his interpretation, that call made the difference in the sense that a friend (his prospective white boss) was doing a favor to a friend (his former white boss).

Some members of minority communities are able to find a job in the formal sector of the economy because there is someone in the institution who sponsors him or her, either because of direct contact (they know each other) or indirect contact (through the brokerage of a friend) or simply because of shared commonalities. A formal letter of recommendation sometimes carries this informal connotation or provides the informal channel through which a minority representative can penetrate the mainstream formal system.

The law of 'credit transfer' means that a mainstreamer will be accepted by a minority community or institution to the extent that he or she is able to transfer credit earned from previous association with a minority person or minority institution.[3] His past engagement is the talisman that leads to further acceptance elsewhere. Here the informal recommendation sometimes carries a formal connotation. This can be accomplished informally, for example, by mentioning the name of the person or organization for which work was previously done. The same rule that the friend of a friend is a potential friend applies here as well.

Case 4. A white woman activist in San Francisco attributes her acceptance by a Chicano organization to the fact that she had volunteered her time while working for a Latino organization on the East Coast. When she came to San Francisco, she simply mentioned the names of a few people she worked for and she was immediately welcomed by the group as a 'sister'. In other words, she had already proved herself as someone who has at heart the well-being of the Chicano community.

These laws, taken together, provide us with a background frame of reference to further understand the influence of informal practices on inter-ethnic relations.

FORMAL FAÇADE AND INFORMAL PRACTICE

The mainstream system defines the minority system as existing in the interstices or on the margins of the mainstream, but in any case as occupying a subjugated position. The ways of the minority system must be distorted to adapt to the norms of the majority system. The formal system is the dominant system, and the minority-formal and two informal systems emerge from it: the mainstream-informal and the minority-informal.

The formal façade is constantly being shaped by the informal reality of practice. The formal façade is the locus for formal interaction, but formal actors also have informal behaviors. In what ways does the informal influence the formal system of inter-ethnic relations?

Case 5. A Chinese-American who is now working in San Francisco said that he used to date a white girlfriend when he was attending college. Their relations were based on personal attraction and common interests and ethnicity was not a major issue for him. All of that changed in his senior year after he had had an informal conversation with two friend room-mates. He made up his mind not to pursue the relationship, based on information he had gained in the informal encounters with his friends.

The informal arena is the locus where ingredients for formal interaction are worked out, where socialization takes place, where strategies to handle the formal are developed, and where solutions are found for problems created in the formal arena. In other words, the study of the formal arena of inter-ethnic relations cannot provide all the clues to understand the everyday operation of formal interactional practices and patterns. A focus on the informal arena, as we stated earlier, is important as well because the informal arena can either hinder or facilitate the management of the formal interaction.

We learn many things that influence our behavior through informal interactions with friends. Some of our naked thoughts, those we cannot discuss in public or in front of strangers, may be voiced among friends. Thus the informal arena is the site where our view of the 'other' (positive or negative) is discussed and nurtured. Subsequently, views learned in the informal arena are carried with us and influence our formal interaction with others. The formal arena may then serve as a laboratory to discredit these views, to test them, or to change them if better information emerges or in response to better acquaintanceship with the 'other'.

The informal arena is also the locus where stereotypes can be reinforced or challenged and rejected. Negative encounters in the formal arena are sometimes carried over to the informal, where they are amplified through informal conversation and gossip. Positive encounters can be reinforced in the same way in the informal arena.

Thus, the informal arena can reinforce or negate views learned and held in the formal arena. This is why we propose the informal arena as a key variable to understanding the formal arena. It is where we strengthen or weaken views held in the formal arena. The informal and formal arenas are revealed as two poles of the same continuum.

FORMAL RULE AND INFORMAL PRACTICE

Society has its formal rules for social interaction. These rules may be remembered, but are not always followed in the conduct of our daily life. However, they place boundaries on the content of our informal practices as these informal practices may be the outcome of a negotiated process.

In social interaction between members of different ethnic groups, when an individual practices the rules put forward by the formal system and the interacting person expresses an informal behavior, there are three types of interaction that may emerge. At one extreme a complete lack of communication may result because the two parties are not on the same wavelength, and misunderstanding arises. Expectations from both sides are not met. Charges of sexism, racism or any other form of bigotry may be levelled at one party or the other in this interaction. The second possible outcome is an interaction with a mixed result. The two people do interact, but the distance or the disjuncture between them may remain. The minority party may see the interaction as paternalistic or feel dominated. In the best of cases, a breakdown of social barriers may result as they meet halfway to make each other feel at home and at ease.

INFORMAL RULE AND FORMAL PRACTICE

Rules for formal behavior are often learned in the informal arena. Once learned there they reinforce our formal practice. One can think of the in-coming secretary who inquires about the ways of the boss so as to better serve his or her needs. This information is learned not through formal training, but rather through informal means.

Even in a situation where informal behavior is called for, an individual may continue to behave formally or to follow formal rules. In such an informal setting the formal practice will be 'naturalized' in a sea of informality to meet informal requirements. Because of the strength of informal rule in this case, formal behavior may not be an obstacle to informal interaction.

Interaction occurs at both the formal level and at the informal level, and progress made informally can be transferred to or have implications for the formal sphere. Informal practices do not simply reject or reinforce ethnic ideas held in the formal arena, but there are circumstances where mainstream members interact directly with the minority informal system and vice versa. The side that initiates the process tends to have the upper hand in the interaction as it may negotiate from a position of strength. Thus, informal practices may not simply influence but may also have the power to transform formal behaviors in the formal sector as informal power may be expressed in very subtle ways.

MINORITY VERSUS MAJORITY

The formal – informal distinction becomes crucial to our understanding of the reproduction of minority status and the ensuing inter-ethnic relations. The minority community is a subordinated site of power and a site of struggle against the total assimilation of the ethnic community by the mainstream system. This power struggle is manifested through grassroots politics and the rise of informal leaders, as well as through the development of an economic and cultural niche catering to the needs of the local community. Asymmetric relations with the mainstream system allow the reproduction of this subsystem.

The minority community is always adjusting to the formal system perceived as being driven by Euro-Americans, even if the municipal leaders come from both majority and minority communities and regardless of the belief that we live in a system of representative democracy. Policies created by the formal system directly affect the minority system in a number of ways. However, this is not a one-way adjustment. Pressures exerted by the minority subsystem have also forced the majority system to adjust to the demands of the minorities.

The major constraint that defines, constructs and reproduces the minority is the power vested in the mainstream system. This is not raw power, but power that is culturally based and tending to be more exclusive than inclusive. It is exclusive in the sense that the mainstream formulates its rules. Although the rules look at the good of the total system, they are, however, culturally produced and consequently biased. The mainstream provides its own vision and cultural definition of society – the system is therefore open to those who agree to play by the formal rules.

Coalition building by which the majority maintains control over the process and the minorities seek to redress the order of things is also imbued with informality. The process of recruitment as well as of interaction is achieved and nurtured in an informal way.

A time factor also helps one to understand the variability in the majority–minority interface. In this light, one may distinguish the soft/wild structure from the hard/settled structure. The soft/wild structure is an unsettled structure where the minority can get in as the structure is being settled. In contrast, a hard/settled structure is more difficult to get into. Here a sponsor or mentor may be needed, as discussed earlier. Acquiring one is not easy, because informality comes in here as well. Such a relationship implies similarity of purpose, background and practice: a friend of a friend, someone belonging to the same club or the same church, or an alumnus from the same school.

The movement of the minority from the ethnic community to the mainstream is a movement from group identity to individual identity as far as the minority person is concerned. He is being individualized by entering the institutions of the mainstream. But it does not work like that from the standpoint of the majority.

The individual is still seen by the mainstream as part of the minority group and therefore cannot escape that status. As a consequence, the inability of the minority representative to be part of the informal network of the dominant group (inner circle) keeps him an outsider, reinforcing his minority status. That he can continue to participate in the informal practices of his ethnic group also reinforces his outsider status *vis-à-vis* the mainstream system and helps reproduce his minority status as well. The minority representative reasons that from the perspective of the majority there is no escape possible (short of a collective protest or revolution) from his subjugated status and the stigma attached to it.

TERRITORIAL SEGREGATION OR ETHNIC ENCLAVES

The ethnic enclave provides a territorial basis where informal practices grow up.[4] Although the minority member may interact with the majority at the formal level, he returns to his community to interact informally there.

Although the enclave may provide a sense of community and a place where the ethnic heritage is nurtured, it can, however, also be an obstacle to inter-ethnic interaction (1) because there is a cultural tradition in the minority ethnic community based on folk perception that may outlive any effort at perceptual change, (2) peers are nearby and reinforce one's sense of belonging to an ethnic community, and (3) the ethnic enclave as an arena for informal practices may be less palatable to outsiders because of the overwhelming majority of ethnic people to be found there.

Enclaves lead to the nurturing of different informal practices in both the majority and minority communities. And indirectly since these practices inform formal behaviors, they are bound to have an impact on the formal system.

INFORMAL PRACTICES AS A WAY OF EMPOWERING
MINORITY PEOPLE

It is often understood that minority people follow informal channels to better empower themselves, to consolidate and discuss their preferences, and to present an enlightened front *vis-à-vis* the mainstream system. This strategy is followed as a way to return to the formal system and to be in a better position to interact with it. It is a retreat strategy implying a separation from the formal system, a recruitment of people to participate in the informal network, an informal communication so as to share ideas, and the will to return to the formal to accomplish one's stated goal.

The operation is not limited to minority ethnic groups: the same strategy can be used by people of any ethnic background. It becomes ethnic when these strategies are developed by any ethnic group for the purpose of distinguishing them from other individuals. If the people who are doing it are from the majority group, the operation is seen as a way of consolidating power or restricting access to the minorities. When it is done by members of a minority ethnic group, it is interpreted as a way of empowering the ethnic participants.

UNCONSCIOUS AND CONSCIOUS IDENTITY

The informal arena also has its influences on the shaping of ethnic identities. It allows an individual to wear a different mask depending on whether he is interacting with people of his own group or outsiders. While the informal arena allows one to be more relaxed and truthful among friends, the formal arena provides a more rigid setting for inter-ethnic relations.

The informal arena provides a niche for the rise and split of the unconscious and conscious identity. An individual can have a discourse or a behavior that he displays in formal interactions with members of other ethnic groups. The same individual may display a different behavior once he is among members of his own group and is able to interact informally with them. Sometimes what one learns in the informal arena tells us more about a situation or an individual than what we learn in the formal arena. The informal arena provides a ground where the informal and unconscious identity of the individual comes to the fore. In this psychological context, one may say that informality is to formality what the unconscious is to the conscious in Freudian psychoanalytic theory.

THE THEORY OF FORMAL/INFORMAL INTER-ETHNIC RELATIONS

The theory identifies four points of juncture: the mainstream-formal, the minority-formal, the mainstream-informal and the minority-informal. The formal is the locus where formal encounters occur. The mainstream-formal and the mainstream-informal are usually more in harmonious relation than the mainstream-formal and the minority-informal. The minority-formal is more in harmony with the minority-informal than with the mainstream-informal while the mainstream-informal is not necessarily in direct relations with the minority-informal. Since these two are not in relational harmony and since they influence the formal, it is likely the actors from both informals (mainstream and minority) may not be in harmonious relation either.

The theory argues that what goes on in the formal arena can often be explained by what goes on in the informal arena. The formal arena provides a site where these interactions occur. However, these interactions can be strengthened or undermined by informal practices that the mainstream and the ethnic community are engaged in. Because of the sheer importance of these informal practices, because of the way they influence formal practices, and because they provide a site where the mainstream differentiates itself from the minority and vice versa, the informal arena is a key factor that must be taken into consideration in order to understand the mechanisms and social construction of inter-ethnic relations.

In the following model (as illustrated in Figure 7.1) we spell out the structural features of the theory:

(1) The informal arena can either consolidate or undermine ethnic interactions in the formal arena. In either situation, it does have an impact on the formal sector and this cannot be ignored if we want to understand the formal domain.
(2) The informal arena provides a locus that feeds the formal practices of inter-ethnic relations and interaction. There is an ongoing feedback between the formal and the informal spheres.

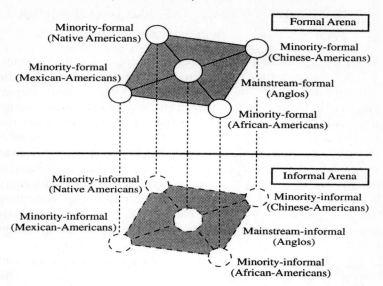

Fig. 7.1 Inter-ethnic relations

(3) Formal interaction cannot be decoded *in toto* without paying attention to the informal realm.

(4) Inequality is manufactured through the asymmetry of social relations nurtured by the formal/informal interface. Informality is seen here both as a site for social control (for the majority), for resistance (for the minorities) and for adaptation (for both).

(5) Gender inequality as manifested in the formal arena is also manufactured daily as a result of the formal/informal interface. Informal practices are used by mainstream males not only to control minorities but women as well. Both women and minorities employed in formal firms are often barred from informal meetings where decisions concerning them are nurtured, discussed, contemplated and adopted.

(6) The minority-formal arena must be distinguished from the mainstream-formal arena. The former is a social site that legitimates itself for social interaction with the latter. It is fed by

whatever goes on in the minority-informal arena and serves as a platform where formal challenges to the status quo can take shape. It is through the minority-formal arena that status enhancement of the minority group and demands for equality are negotiated.

The theory proposes that creation of true harmony in the formal sphere depends on several factors:

(1) The mainstream-informal should cease to be the hidden side of the formal, so that all actors may be on the same footing at the formal level and everyone may be privy to all pertinent information necessary to be an insider. Unfortunately this is not possible.
(2) Minorities should be equally represented at the formal level as a way of providing some balance in the formal interaction and in the production of national and hegemonic ideologies. This may be possible through social engineering, and therefore can be proposed as a realistic solution.
(3) The mainstream-informal should become a minority-informal as well so that the mainstream-formal may be equally representative of both. This is not practical because of cultural differences and the ethnic stratification in the power system.
(4) Given the actual structure and the difficulty of minoritizing the informal-mainstream, more harmonious relations and interaction should occur between the two informals. This is done at the individual level, but not routinely at the group level.
(5) The optimum solution should be total integration, which means here the division of society into an integrated formal and integrated informal. This idealistic 'melting pot' solution is not practical either because of the desire of most people to cling to their ethnic groups.
(6) A more workable solution should take into consideration the reality of ethnic diversity and the requirements of representative democracy as the best way to get out of the dilemma.

Inter-ethnic relations in the present social structure of the San Francisco Bay Area tend to reproduce inequality. The problem is located in the asymmetry of relations which are used by the formal (site of power) to dominate (politics), control (legal apparatus), coerce (police), make inferior (identity), subjugate (economy) and marginalize (space) ethnic minority practices.

The group that decides which system is formal and which one is not has the upper hand in the equation. It makes the rules while other people must follow them, often to their disadvantage simply because they must adapt to someone else's agenda. In this way, the minorities participate or take part in the operation that reproduces over time their minority status. Thus, the phenomenon of ethnogenesis is an ongoing process whereby subjugated ethnic minorities attempt through various forms of struggle and resistance to overcome informalization of their cultural ways and institutions as well as undermine the asymmetry of their relations with the dominant sector of society.

Notes

1. There is a vast literature on inter-ethnic relations dealing with the manifestation of the phenomenon on the urban American scene. For a glimpse at the various theoretical shades and methodological orientations of this literature, see Takaki (1987).

2. Michel Foucault's (1980) seminal work on the technology of power serves as a source of inspiration for my interpretation of the interface between formality and informality.

3. I am indebted to Professor Leonard Duhl of the Public Health Department at Berkeley for sharing this observation with me.

4. For descriptions of the historical evolution of ethnic enclaves in San Francisco, see Godfrey (1988) and Wirt (1974). Monographs on specific ethnic groups in San Francisco are also available; see Daniels (1980) on African-Americans, Narell (1981) on Jews, Nee and Nee (1972), Chow (1977) and Loo (1991) on Chinese, Gumina (1978) and Cinel (1982) on Italians, Decroos (1983) on Basques, Burchell (1979) on the Irish, Tripp (1980) on Russians and Leyland (1980) on Puerto Ricans.

8

Conclusion

As we arrive at the end of our reflections on the nature and the polivocality of the informal city as canvassed through our examination of the everyday practices in the San Francisco Bay Area, we believe that the approach allows us to study a hidden dimension that sheds much light on our comprehension of the formal city. This approach is not only important to understanding informal factors that shape the behavior of the formal city, but also informs us on the nature of the relations between these two poles of the social system, and more specifically on the way the informal system behaves. Probably one of the most revealing aspects of the enterprise is that it shows us how important it is to factor in *human agency* in our understanding of urban processes.

THE MULTIVOCALITY OF INFORMALITY

One of the major issues in the study of the informal city is the difficulty in identifying and locating the object of study. That would not have been the case if it were a separate reality in a dual system. In fact, it is a contingent reality in a unified system. Its study cannot be divorced from that of the formal system since it is the other side and in some cases the lifeblood of that system.

Another difficulty stems from the flexibility and fluidity of the informal system. It does not have a rigid structure, or even a permanent one, and is activated by the actors of the formal system. This fluidity allows it to move back and forth in the formal system and to disintegrate or occupy a marginal position at times as it allows the formal system to pursue its course of action.

I have come to realize that urban informality is not monolithic and that it presents itself in different shapes and forms. In its internal behavior, urban informality can be identified as having singular characteristics, some of which I delineate below because

157

of their importance in relation with other informal units of the informal city and with the formal city as well.

Urban informality is found to be *competitive*. By that is meant that 'informality may come about through the efforts of firms and other private interests in a regulated economy to gain market advantage by avoiding some state controls' (Portes *et al.*, 1989: 299). It is a means used to take advantage of or move to a competitive edge against competitors in various domains of social life. It is a mechanism used to outdo a competitor. We see it at work in the realm of the formal industry where informal professionals are hired in order to lower costs, and in the moderately regulated Stock Exchange in the case of insider trading where those who are privy to such knowledge reposition themselves favorably in the formal market system at the expense of competitors.

Urban informality can be *altruistic*. It is used as a way of maximizing the well-being of others. One uses an informal communication line to help another person. An individual sometimes gets a job not simply on the basis of formal procedure, but also of informal things that go on, for example a telephone call by a friendly third party to the employer.

Urban informality can be *reciprocal*. It is used as a way to maintain an exchange process. *Reciprocity* is the key to understanding the intention of the act. An informal behavior is materialized to help someone who may be able to return the favor.

Urban informality is either *latent* or *active*. It is latent when a learned behavior or a practice remains in a dormant state and therefore can be activated at any moment for a specific purpose. It is active when the informal behavior is used to accomplish stated ends.

Urban informality is *routinized* when it is part of one's daily life. This routinization process consists of meshing together both formal and informal activities in such a way that the informal is perceived as something integral to the process of everyday life.

Urban informality can also be *transformative*. Transformative informality is understood to be informal behavior expressed with a view to changing any aspect of the formal social reality.

Urban informality is found to have a *symbolic* dimension. Symbolic informality is behavior expressed for the clear purpose of projecting a symbolic image of oneself. It can be used as an indicator of class status through participation in an informal group in order to enhance one's image in society.

Urban informality is at times *discriminatory*. Discriminatory informality is an informal practice that excludes certain people from participation in an informal group meeting. Segregation is a characteristic of raw informality while integration is a characteristic of cooked informality. If informality can be discriminatory, there are also instances where it becomes *integrative*.

The role of the informal arena as the locus where formal activities are discussed informally before formal action is taken or as a way to guide formal action points to the integration of the formal city in its formal and informal aspects.

Urban informality tends to strengthen class divisions as it is used to consolidate group interests and to discriminate against outsiders. On the other hand, it also serves as a mechanism for upward mobility as it allows people of different classes to partake in communal informal activities.

Urban informality can also be *subversive* because it provides a structure of resistance. According to Harding and Jenkins (1989: 136) 'the power of formal regulations creates the possibility of its subversion'. The formal system creates *substitutive* informality so that it can continue to function smoothly. Substitutive informality is a pillar of the formal system because of its safety-valve function.

This function as a safety valve can be seen in its role as an extension of formality, but it also provides an arena where formal problems can be discussed informally and informal solutions can be found.

The safety-valve function also provides an arena where dissidents plot out their strategies to undermine or subvert the formal system. This subversive function is latent and comes into play in times of crisis or revolution, here defined in terms of a vast density of *subversive* informality that undermines the ability of the formal system to maintain its cohesion.

INFORMAL/FORMAL RELATIONS

The idea and reality of informality implies both an active and passive relation *vis-à-vis* the formal domain. In the active sense, it is a reality that is repressed by the formal system thus preventing it from being 'formal'. In the passive sense, it is an activity that is 'out there' and one which the formal system does not pretend to or cannot control. In both its active and passive meanings, informality is seen as being capable of having an impact on the formal system.

This study of informal practices has been carried out at three different levels. The first level is that of direct observation, as the same individuals who engage in formal practices are also engaged in informal practices. The second level is that of the transformation (migration or co-optation) of informal practices into formal practices, as when folk remedies are adopted by the modern medical hospital and transformed into pharmaceutical drugs. And the third level is that of the transformation of some formal practices into informal practices because they have lost their formal identity, as in the case of the street vendor whose licence has been revoked by the state.

We conceive of the formal system as comprising several spaces where formal and informal activities occur either simultaneously or successively. The informal system is included in the larger formal space.

The reality of informality is seen as related to the topography of the formal societal system and constitutes a province of that system. When the informal system is recouped by the formal, it becomes a layer of that system and may be located in a hierarchy of subsystem. As such it constitutes a hidden force within the formal system.

The relations of informality to formality are spelled out in terms of the structural organization of the overall system. The informal system is seen as an *adaptation* to the formal system because it may be produced by the formal system and its survival depends on the existence of the formal system. Consequently changes in the formal system may induce changes in the informal system.

The informal system is also seen as a *reaction* to the formal system, especially when this is superimposed. Such was the case in the formation of slave religion. To the *action* of the formal system corresponds the *reaction* of the informal system, or to a formal structure of domination may correspond an informal structure of resistance.

The informal system appears also as a *challenge* to the formal system. For example, the traffic of drugs in the streets of the city challenges formal authorities to do something about it.

The informal system appears as a *substitution* for what is missing in the formal system. For example, street vendors satisfy the consumer needs of a number of people. They sell cheap, fast and handy goods that are not provided by the formal system.

The informal system is *complementary* to formal institutions. This is the case in the widespread use of folk medicine among the African-American, Chinese and Hispanic communities in the San Francisco Bay Area that fulfills needs not met by modern medicine or the modern hospital.

THE REPRODUCTION OF HEGEMONY

Although all the social classes participate in informal practices, it is true to say that they help reproduce inequality and hierarchy in society. Those of the upper class sometimes use informality to maintain their position and to exclude outsiders from their inner circles. Being at the top, they have access to more influential people than the other classes. At the same time, urban informality is used by some lower-and middle-class individuals as a means to upward mobility as it provides an avenue for penetrating influential circles.

The notion of informality is at the very center of the Western project of the construction and the strengthening of the democratic state. Can the democratic system be totally open and transparent in any society where urban informality reigns supreme? It seems at first that because informal practices tend to discriminate against those who are not invited to join in they are an impediment to the achievement of equality, fairness and perhaps democracy.

Because informality allows individuals to take a shortcut and gives advantages to some over others based on class, gender, ethnicity, religion or political affiliation, it tends to reproduce inequality in society. It is a well lubricated engine in the social reproduction of hegemonic practices and at the same time it is an arena exploited to prevent direct group confrontations. Perhaps one may conclude that informal practices are both a productive device and an enlightening paradox in the texture of the American city.

References

Abel, R. *The Politics of Informal Justice* (New York: Academic Press, 1982).

Akinnaso, F.N. Schooling, Language, and Knowledge in Literate and Nonliterate Societies. *Comparative Studies in Society and History*, Vol. 34, No. 1 (1992), pp. 68–109.

Alexander, M.J. *Information Systems Analysis: Theory and Applications* (Chicago: Science Research Associates Inc., 1974).

Archambault, E. and Greffe, X. *Les Economies Non Officielles* (Paris: Editions La Découverte, 1984).

Auerback, J. *Justice Without Law* (New York: Oxford University Press, 1983).

Barnard, C.I. *The Functions of the Executive* (Cambridge, Mass.: Harvard University Press, 1958).

Becquart-Leclercq, J. Relational Power and Systemic Articulation in French Local Polity. In Karpik, L. (ed.), *Organization and Environment: Theory, Issues and Reality* (London: Sage Publications, 1978), pp. 253–92.

Becquart-Leclercq, J. *La Démocratie Locale à l'Américaine* (Paris: Presses Universitaires de France, 1988).

Benton, L. *The Role of the Informal Sector in Economic Development: Industrial Restructuring in Spain*. PhD dissertation, Department of Anthropology, Johns Hopkins University, 1986.

Benton, L.A. *Invisible Factories: The Informal Economy and Industrial Development in Spain* (Albany, NY: State University of New York Press, 1990).

Blau, P.M. *Exchange and Power in Social Life* (New York: Wiley, 1964).

Blau, P.M. *The Dynamics of Bureaucracy* (Chicago: University of Chicago Press, 1964).

Blocker, C.E. and Schauer, C.H. *The Formal and Informal Structures of a College and a Business Organization: An Analysis* (Harrisburg, Pa. 1965).

Boer, L. Informalization: The Forces Beyond. *International Journal of Urban and Regional Research*, Vol. 14, No. 3 (1990), pp. 404–22.

Bourdieu, P. *Outline of a Theory of Practice* (New York: Cambridge University Press, 1990).

Britan, G. and Cohen, R. (eds) *Hierarchy and Society* (Philadelphia: Institute for the Study of Human Issues, 1980).

Browning, R.P., Rogers Marshall, D. and Tabb, D.H. *Protest is not Enough: The Struggle of Blacks and Hispanics for Equality in Urban Politics* (Berkeley, Calif.: University of California Press, 1984).

Bullough, B. and Bullough, V.L. *Poverty, Ethnic Identity and Health Care* (New York: Appleton-Century-Crofts, 1972).

Burchell, R.A. *The San Francisco Irish, 1848–1880* (Manchester: Manchester University Press, 1979).

Carlson, R.O. Informal Organization and Social Distance: A Paradox of Purposive Organization. *Educational Administration and Supervision*, Vol. XLIV, No. 6 (November 1958).

Castells, M. *The Informational City* (Cambridge: Basil Blackwell, 1989).

Castells, M. and Portes, A. World Underneath: The Origins, Dynamics and Effects of the Informal Economy. In Portes, A. (ed.), *The Informal Economy* (Baltimore, Md.: Johns Hopkins University Press, 1989), pp. 11–37.

Chisholm, D. *Coordination Without Hierarchy: Informal Structures in Multi-organizational Systems* (Berkeley, Calif.: University of California Press, 1989).

Chow, W.T. *The Re-Emergence of an Inner-City: The Pivot of Chinese Settlement in the East Bay Region of the San Francisco Bay Area* (San Francisco: R. & E. Associates, 1977).

Cinel, D. *From Italy to San Francisco: The Immigrant Experience* (Palo Alto, Calif.: Stanford University Press, 1982).

Clark, G. (ed.) *Traders versus the State: Anthropological Approaches to Unofficial Economies* (Boulder, Colo.: Westview Press, 1988).

Comeau, Y. Resurgence de la Vie Quotidienne et de ses Sociologies. *Sociologie et Société*, Vol. 19, No. 2 (1987), pp. 115–23.

Cook, K. *et al.* (eds) *The Limits of Rationality* (Chicago: University of Chicago Press, 1990).

Crenson, M.A. *Neighborhood Politics* (Cambridge, Mass.: Harvard University Press, 1983).

Cuff, D. *Architecture: The Story of Practice* (Cambridge, Mass.: MIT Press, 1991).

Dalton, M. *Men Who Manage. Fusions of Feeling and Theory in Administration* (New York: John Wiley, 1959).

Daniels, D.H. *Pioneer Urbanites: A Social and Cultural History of Black San Francisco* (Philadelphia, Pa.: Temple University Press, 1980).

Davies, R. *The Informal Sector: A Solution to Unemployment* (London: Catholic Institute for International Relations, 1978).

Davis, J. Forms and Norms: The Economy of Social Relations. *Man*, Vol. 8, No. 2 (1973), pp. 159–76.

Davis, K. Management Communication and the Grapevine. *Harvard Business Review*, Vol. XXXI (1953), pp. 43–9.

De Certeau, M. *The Practice of Everyday Life* (Berkeley, Calif.: University of California Press, 1984).

De Soto, H. *The Other Path: The Invisible Revolution in the Third World* (New York: Harper & Row, 1990).

de Tocqueville, A. Democracy in America (New York: Vintage Books, 1945).

Decroos, J.F. *The Long Journey: Social Integration and Ethnicity Maintenance among Urban Basques in the San Francisco Bay Area Region* (Reno, Nev.: Associated University Press, 1983).

Duchacek, J. The International Dimension of Subnational Self-Government. *Publius*, Vol. 4 (1984), pp. 5–31.

Durkheim, E. *Professional Ethics and Civic Morals* (Glencoe, Ill.: Free Press, 1960).

Ellis, W.R., Chao T., and Parrish, J. Levi's Place: A Building Biography. *Places*, Vol. 2, No. 1 (1985), pp. 57–70.

Etzioni, A. Two Approaches to Organizational Analysis: A Critique and a Suggestion. In Grusky, O. and Miller, G.A. (eds), *The Sociology of Organizations* (London: Free Press, 1970), pp. 215–25.

Fairhurst, G.T. and Snavely, B.K. Majority and Token Minority Group Relationships: Power Acquisition and Communication. *Academy of Management Review*, Vol. 8 (1983), pp. 292–300.

Ferman, L.A. *et al*. *The Informal Economy* (Beverly Hills, Calif.: Sage, 1987).

Fischer, C.S. *To Dwell Among Friends: Personal Networks in Town and City* (Chicago: University of Chicago Press, 1982).

Fitzpatrick, P. The Rise and Rise of Informalism. In Matthews, R. (ed.), *Informal Justice* (London: Sage, 1988), pp. 178–98.

Foucault, M. *Power/Knowledge* (New York: Pantheon, 1980).

Freidson, E. *Patients' Views of Medical Practice* (New York: Russell Sage Foundation, 1961).

Freidson, E. *Profession of Medicine: A Study of the Sociology of Applied Knowledge* (Chicago: The University of Chicago Press, 1988).

Giddens, A. *The Constitution of Society* (Berkeley, Calif.: University of California Press, 1984).

Godfrey, B.J. *Neighborhoods in Transition: The Making of San Francisco's Ethnic and Nonconformist Communities* (Berkeley, Calif.: University of California Press, 1988).

Goffman, E. *The Presentation of Self in Everyday Life* (New York: Doubleday Anchor Books, 1959).

Goffman, E. *Asylums: Essays on the Social Situation of Mental Patients and Other Inmates* (New York: Doubleday Anchor Books, 1961).

Goffman, E. *Behavior in Public Places* (New York: Free Press, 1963).

Goffman, E. *Interaction Ritual* (London: Allen Lane, 1972).

Gottdiener, M. *The Social Production of Urban Space* (Austin, Tex.: University of Texas Press, 1988).

Gould-Martin, K. and Ngin C. Chinese Americans. In Harwood, A. (ed.), *Ethnicity and Medical Care* (Cambridge, Mass.: Harvard University Press, (1981), pp. 130–71.

Gouldner, A.W. *Patterns of Industrial Bureaucracy* (New York: Free Press, 1954).

Graham, H. Providers, Negotiators and Mediators: Women as the Hidden Carers. In Lewin, E. and Olesen, V. (eds), *Women, Health and Healing: Towards a New Perspective* (London: Tavistock, 1985), pp. 25–52.

Greer, S. and Orleans, P. The Mass Society and the Parapolitical Structure. *American Sociological Review*, Vol. 27, No. 5 (1962), pp. 634–46.

Gross, B.M. The Scientific Approach to Administration. In Griffiths, D. (ed.), *Behavioral Science and Educational Administration* (Chicago: University of Chicago Press, 1964), pp. 33–72.

Guest, A.M. and Oropesa, R.S. Informal Social Ties and Political Activity in the Metropolis. *Urban Affairs Quarterly*, Vol. 21, No. 4 (1986) pp. 550–74.

Gumina, D.P. *The Italians of San Francisco, 1850–1930* (New York: Center for Migration Studies, 1978).

Hall, E. *The Hidden Dimension* (New York: Doubleday, 1966).

Hall, O. The Informal Organization of the Medical Profession. *The Canadian Journal of Economics and Political Science*, Vol. 12, No. 1 (1946), pp. 30–44.

Hamilton, C.V. *The Black Preacher in America* (New York: William Morrow, 1972).

Harding, P. and Jenkins, R. *The Myth of the Hidden Economy: Towards a New Understanding of Informal Economic Activity* (Philadelphia, Pa.: Open University Press, 1989).

Hart, K. Informal Income Opportunities and Urban Employment in Ghana. *Journal of Modern African Studies*, Vol. 11 (1973), pp. 61–89.

Hayes, E.C. *Power Structure and Urban Policy: Who Rules in Oakland?* (New York: McGraw-Hill, 1972).

Henry, S. *Informal Institutions: Adaptive Networks in the Corporate State* (New York: St. Martin's Press, 1981).

Herzfeld, M. The Poeticity of the Commonplace. *Semiotic Theory and Practice*, Vol. 1 (1988), pp. 383–91.

Iannaccone, L. An Approach to the Informal Organization of the School. In Griffiths, D.E. (ed.), *Behavioral Science and Educational Administration* (Chicago: University of Chicago Press, (1964) pp. 223–42.

Johnston, J.C. *Informal Organization: A Transitional Force in Formal Organization Structure*. Master of Business Administration, University of California at Berkeley, California, 1954.

Jones, Y.V. Street Peddlers as Entrepreneurs: Economic Adaptation to an Urban Area. *Urban Anthropology*, Vol.17 (1988), pp. 143–70

Kanter, R.M. *Men and Women of the Corporation* (New York: Basic Books, 1977).

Knoke, D. *Political Networks:The Structural Perspective* (New York: Cambridge University Press, 1990).

Kolb, D.M. and Bartunek, J.M. (eds), *Hidden Conflict in Organizations: Uncovering Behind-the-Scenes Disputes* (Newbury Park, Calif.: Sage, 1992).

Lanzetta de Pardo, M. *et al.* The Articulation of Formal and Informal Sectors in the Economy of Bogotá, Columbia. In Portes, A. *et al.* (eds), *The Informal Economy* (Baltimore, Conn.: Johns Hopkins University Press, 1989), pp. 95–110.

Lefebvre, H. *La Production de l'Espace* (Paris: Anthropos, 1974).

Levin, L.S. and Idler, E.D. *The Hidden Health Care System: Mediating Structures and Medicine* (Cambridge, Mass.: Ballinger, 1981).

Leyland, R.C. *Puerto Ricans in the San Francisco Bay Area, California: A Historical and Cultural Geography*. Master's Thesis, Department of Geography, California State University at Hayward, 1980.

Logan, J.R. and Molotch, H.L. *Urban Fortunes: The Political Economy of Place* (Berkeley, Calif.: University of California Press, 1987).

Lomnitz, L.A. Informal Exchange Networks in Formal Systems: A Theoretical Model. *American Anthropologist*, Vol. 90, No. 1 (1988), pp. 42–55.

Loo, C.M. *Chinatown: Most Time, Hard Time* (New York: Praeger, 1991).

Lozano, B.A. High Technology, Cottage Industry: A Study of Informal Work in the San Francisco Bay Area. PhD Dissertation, University of California at Davis.

Lozano, B. Informal Sectors Workers:Walking Out the Systems's Front Door. *International Journal of Urban and Regional Research*, Vol. 7, No. 3 (1983), pp. 340–61.

Lozano, B. *The Invisible Work Force* (New York: Free Press, 1989).

McDowell, L. Towards an Understanding of the Gender Division of Urban Space. *Society and Space*, Vol. 1 (1983), pp. 59–72.

MacKenzie, S. Neglected Spaces in Peripheral Places: Home-Workers and the Creation of a New Economic Center. *Cahiers de Geographie du Québec*, Vol. 13, No. 83 (1987), pp. 247–60.

Maffesoli, M. The Sociology of Everyday Life (Epistemological Elements). *Current Sociology*, Vol. 37, No. 1 (1989), pp. 1–16.

Masson, D. Les Femmes dans Les Structures Urbaines: Apercu d'un Nouveau Champ de Recherche. *Revue Canadienne des Sciences Politiques*, Vol. 17, No. 4 (1984), pp. 754–82.

Matthews, R. (ed.) *Informal Justice* (London: Sage, 1988).

Mauss, M. *Essai sur le Don* (London: Cohen & West, 1954).

Merton, R.K. *Social Theory and Social Structure* (Glencoe, Ill.: Free Press, 1961).

Meyrowitz, J. *No Sense of Place: The Impact of Electronic Media on Social Behavior* (New York: Oxford University Press, 1985).

Mittar, V. *Growth of Urban Informal Sector in a Developing Economy* (New Delhi: Deep and Deep Publications, 1988).

Moore, H.L. *Feminism and Anthropology* (Minneapolis: University of Minnesota Press, 1988).

Narell, I. *Our City: The Jews of San Francisco* (San Diego Calif.: Howell-North Books, 1981).

Nee, V.G. and de Bary Nee, B. *Longtime Californ': A Documentary Study of an American Chinatown* (New York: Pantheon Books, 1972).

Nicholson, L.J. (ed.) *Feminism/Postmodernism* (New York: Routledge, 1990).

Nilles, J. *The Telecommunications-Transportation Trade-Off: Options for Tomorrow* (New York: Wiley, 1976).

Papola, T.S. *Urban Informal Sector in a Developing Economy* (Delhi: Vikas, 1981).

Portes, A. *et al. The Informal Economy* (Baltimore, Conn.: Johns Hopkins University Press, 1989).

Roethlisberger, F.J. and Dickson, W.J. *Management and the Worker* (Cambridge, Mass.: Harvard University Press, 1947).

Rojas, J.T. *The Enacted Environment: The Creation of 'Place' by Mexicans and Mexican-Americans in East Los Angeles*. Master of Sciences, Department of Architecture, MIT, 1991.

Rosaldo, M.Z. Woman, Culture and Society: A Theoretical Overview. In Rosaldo, M. *et al.* (eds), *Women, Culture and Society* (Palo Alto, Calif.: Standford University Press, 1974), pp. 17–42.

Rose, R. *Getting by in Three Economies: The Resources of the Official, Unofficial and Domestic Economies.* Studies in Public Policy, No. 110. Glasgow: Centre for the Study of Public Policy, 1983.

Ross, D.P. and Usher, P.J. *From the Roots Up: Economic Development as if Community Mattered.* The Canadian Council on Social Development Series (Toronto: James Lorimer, 1986).

Sack, R.D. *Conception of Space in Social Thought* (Minneapolis: University of Minneapolis Press, 1980).

Santos, B. de S. Law, a Map of Misreading: Toward a Postmodern Conception of Law. *Journal of Law and Society* Vol. 14, No. 3 (1987), pp. 279–302.

Santos, M. *The Shared Space: The Two Circuits of the Urban Economy in Underdeveloped Countries* (New York: Methuen, 1979).

Sassen-Koob, S. New York City's Informal Economy. In Portes, A. *et al.* (ed.), The Informal Economy (Baltimore, Md.: Johns Hopkins University Press, 1989), pp. 60–77.

Sauvy, A. *Le Travail Noir et l'Economie de Demain* (Paris: Calmann-Levy, 1984).

Sayles, L.R. *Human Behavior in Organizations.* Englewood Cliffs, NJ: Prentice-Hall, 1966).

Schiff, F.W. Flexiplace: An Idea Whose Time Has Come. *IEEE Transactions on Engineering Management,* Vol. 30, No. 1 (1983), pp. 26–30.

Schreiber, J.M. and Homiak, J.P. Mexican Americans. In Harwood, A. (ed.), *Ethnicity and Medical Care* (Cambridge, Mass.: Harvard University Press, 1981), pp. 264–336.

Scott, J.C. *Domination and the Arts of Resistance: Hidden Transcripts* (New Haven, Conn.: Yale University Press, 1990).

Selznick, P. An Approach to a Theory of Bureaucracy. In Coser, L.A. and Rosenberg, B. (eds), *Sociological Theory* (New York: Macmillan, 1964), pp. 477–88.

Sethuraman, S.V. *The Urban Informal Sector in Developing Countries: Employment, Poverty and Environment* (Geneva: International Labor Office, 1981).

Shankland, G. *Our Street Economy* (London: Anglo German Foundation for the Study of Industrial Society, 1980).

Sharma, U. *Complementary Medicine Today: Practitioners and Patients* (London: Tavistock, 1992).

Silver, H. The Demand for Homework: Evidence from the U.S. Census. In Boris, E. and Daniels, C.R. (eds), *Homework: Historical and Contemporary Perspectives on Paid Labor at Home* (Urbana, Ill.: University of Illinois Press, 1989), pp. 103–29.

Simon, H.A. *Administrative Behavior* (New York: Macmillan, 1966).

Sitton, T. Inside School Spaces: Rethinking the Hidden Dimension. *Urban Education,* Vol. 15, No. 1 (1980), pp. 65–82.

Smith, M.E. (ed.) *Perspectives on the Informal Economy.* Monographs in Economic Anthropology, No. 8 (Lanham, Va.: University Press of America, 1990).

Smith, S. and Wied-Nebbeling, S. *The Shadow Economy in Britain and Germany* (London: Anglo-German Foundation for the Study of Industrial Society, 1986).

Soldatos, P. Les Relations Internationales du Québec: Une Paradiplomacie à Géométrie Variable. In Monière, D. (ed.), *L'Année Politique au Québec 1988–1989* (Montreal, 1990).

Sommer, R. *Social Design: Creating Buildings With People in Mind* (Englewood Cliffs, NJ: Prentice-Hall, 1983).

Spain, D. *Gendered Spaces* (Chapel Hill, NC: University of North Carolina Press, 1992).

Sutton, H. and Porter A Study of the Grapevine in a Governmental Organization. *Personnel Psychology*, Vol. 21 (1968), pp. 223–30.

Takaki, R. *From Different Shores: Perspectives on Race and Ethnicity in America* (New York: Oxford University Press, 1987).

Tanzi, V. *The Underground Economy in the United States and Abroad* (Lexington, Mass. D.C. Heath, 1982).

Tinker, I. (ed.) Street Food: Testing Assumptions About Informal Sector Activity By Women and Men. *Current Sociology*, Vol. 35, No. 3 (1987).

Toffler, A. *The Third Wave* (New York: William Morrow, 1980).

Tomeh, A.K. Informal Group Participation and Residential Patterns. *American Journal of Sociology*, Vol. 70, No. 1 (1964), pp. 28–35.

Tripp, M.W. *Russian Routes: Origins and Development of an Ethnic Community in San Francisco*. Master's Thesis, Department of Geography, San Francisco State University, 1980.

Turnham, D., Salome, B. and Schwarz, A. (eds) *Nouvelles Approaches du Secteur Informel* (Paris: Centre de Dévelopment de l'Organisation de Coopération et de Développement Economiques, 1990).

Van Dijk, M.P. Sénégal: Le Secteur Informel de Dakar (Paris: L'Harmattan, 1986).

Uzzell, Douglas Dissonance of Formal and Informal Planning Styles, or Can Formal Planners Do Bricolage? *City and Society*, Vol. 4, No. 2 (1990), pp. 114–130.

Wallerstein, I.M. *Capitalist Agriculture and the Origins of the European World Economy in the Sixteenth Century* (New York: Academic Press, 1976).

Wekerle, G., Peterson, R. and Morley, D. *New Space for Women* (Boulder, Colo.: Westview, 1980).

Whyte, W.H. *The Social Life of Small Urban Spaces* (Washington DC: Conversation Foundation, 1980).

Wirt, F.M. *Power in the City: Decision-Making in San Francisco* (Berkeley, Calif.: University of California Press, 1974).

Zelinsky, W. *et al.* Women and Geography: A Review and Prospects. *Progress in Human Geography*, Vol. 6, No. 3 (1982), pp. 317–66.

Zey-Ferrell, M. *Dimensions of Organizations: Environment, Context, Structure, Process, and Performance* (Santa Monica, Calif.: Goodyear, 1979).

Index

Index

DATE DUE

JUL 0 5 1998			